Outing the Church

Outing the Church

40 Years in the
Queer Christian Movement

Rev. Dr. Nancy Wilson

LifeJourney
PRESS

Grateful acknowledgment is made for permission to quote from the following:

Scripture quotations are from the New Revised Standard Version of the Bible, copyright ©1989 by the Division of Christian Education of the National Council of the Churches of Christ in the U.S.A. Used by permission. All rights reserved.

Excerpts from the ANCHOR BIBLE DICTIONARY by David Noel Freedman, Editor. Copyright © 1992 by Doubleday, a division of Bantam Doubleday Dell Publishing Group, Inc. Used by permission of Doubleday, a division of Bantam Doubleday Dell Publishing Group, Inc.

Published in Indianapolis, Indiana, by LifeJourney Press, LifeJourneyPress.cc. Printed in the United States of America.

Editing by Grant E. Mabie.
Book design and layout by David W. Squire.
Editorial support by Keith Phillips and Johnna VanHoose Dinse.

For other products from LifeJourney Press, visit www.LifeJourneyPress.cc.

For information contact:
The Universal Fellowship of the Metropolitan Community Churches
PO Box 50488
Sarasota, Florida 34232 USA
info@MCCchurch.net
Telephone (310) 360-8640 Fax: (310) 388-1252

To Paula, for a wonderful life of love and surprises,
and for listening to all my stories . . .

Set me as a seal upon your heart,

as a seal upon your arm;

for love is strong as death,

passion fierce as the grave.

Its flashes are flashes of fire,

a raging flame.

Many waters cannot quench love,

neither can floods drown it.

If one offered for love

all the wealth of her house,

it would be utterly scorned.

Song of Solomon 8:6–7

Special Contributors

The following generous people participated in a crowdfunding campaign that made publication of these two new books possible.

Because of their generosity, many people across the globe will find a spiritual home in MCC and a message of spiritual hope in the Bible. They have given the gift of spiritual life!

Angela and Irma Bauer-Levesque
Patricia A. Beaver and
    Estella M. Thomas
Toby Bishop and Rev. Kevin Downer
Rev. Houston Burnside Jr.
Gilbert Carrasco and Isai DeLaO
Rev. Marian Cavagnaro
Skip Chasey
Beverly Cotton
Rev. Dee and Judy Dale
Dr. Gail Evans, in memory of
    Rev. Jean R. Hart
Don Ferrell and Ronn Valent
Rev. Darlene Garner and
    Rev. Candy Holmes
Lea A. Harthcock
Julie Krueger
Benjamin N. Lamb
Connie Meadows and
    Haviland Houston
Lee Melvin and Carl Williams
Rev. Vickie Miller and Carol Lidey
Carole L. Murrey
Rev. Elijah C. Nealy

Rev. Jane Nelson and Gay Fritzemeier
Sherrill Parmley
Rev. Troy D. Perry and
    Mr. Phillip Ray De Blieck
Rev. Dr. Keith J. Phillips
Robert W. Pope and
    Lawrence Konrad
Rev. Dusty Pruitt and
    Ms. Joanne Rhodes
Deacon Dar Purugganan
Gail Rissler
Rev. Dr. Joan Saniuk and
    Sharilyn Steketee
Rick Sherwin
Toni L. Smith
David F. Sorey and
    Donald L. Johnson
David Squire and David Wene
E. T. Thomas and Pat Beaver
Rev. Donna Twardowski and
    Marilyn A. Kane
Rev. Robin White and
    Chp. Barry Christensen
Byron Yaple

Contents

Acknowledgments 1

Introduction: Tribal Tales 3

1 • Healing Our Tribal Wounds 15

2 • Boldly Exercising Our Tribal Gifts 33

3 • Seismic Theology 59

4 • Equal to Angels 97

5 • A Queer Theology of Sexuality 115

Notes 153

Subject Index 157

Scripture Index 163

Acknowledgments

In some ways, writing a book is a very solitary thing. In many other ways, though, if you are the pastor of a church, it is not! This book originated in the context of pastoring MCC Los Angeles. Rev. Evelyn Kinser worked with me on the idea of moving from the "defense" to the "offense" in treating the subject of homosexuality in the Bible, which evolved, in the changing political vocabulary of our community, to "Outing the Bible." Evelyn was a constant source of encouragement and challenge to me.

Through moving many times, earthquakes, mortgage woes, and untold grief and loss, I learned from the members, friends, staff, and board of MCC Los Angeles the truth of Psalm 46:

> God is our refuge and strength, a very present help in trouble.
> Therefore we will not fear, though the earth should change,
> though the mountains shake in the heart of the sea.

Thanks to the members of my home church, Church of the Trinity MCC in Sarasota, Florida.

Special thanks to those who assisted in the making of this book: Bless you, Sandy Williams, for trips to the library. Thanks to Linda Brenner-Beckstead for all your help, and to Ann Craig for your encouragement and editing.

This book would not have happened without Fr. Malcolm Boyd. When we were doing a "gig" together in San Francisco, Malcolm told me I had to write this book. You are my fairy godfather!

Thank you, Rev. Troy Perry, for starting MCC; for seeing my potential in those early days; for being an incredibly openhearted, open-minded leader; for being willing to be the prophet of God. Thanks to the MCC Elders—Rev. Darlene Garner, Rev. Mona West, Rev. Lillie Brock, Rev.

Ken Martin, and Rev. Hector Gutierrez—for your partnership in MCC's ministry; and thanks to all who have served MCC as Elders. Thanks to Bishop Yvette Flunder whose partnership is giving birth to whole new possibilities for radical inclusion. And, to Barb Crabtree for saying yes to being our Director of Operations.

Thanks to: Dr. Dusty Pruitt, who offered friendship and support when I so much needed it years ago; and colleagues Rabbi Denise Eger and Rev. Dan Smith for your support and encouragement. Thank you Jean Gralley, artist and friend, especially for my first love letters! Thanks to Rev. Pat Bumgardner, friend and colleague in doing justice.

Thanks to my very diverse family. Thank you, Lori Dick, for wisdom, friendship, and quiet presence. Thanks to: Ravi Verma, my spiritual brother, friend, ally; Terri, Dyan and Hannah Ullman-Levine, for safety and home and friendship; my mother, Barbara Wilson, for your encouragement and love; brother Mark; the Chase clan; my other Mom, Marian Schoenwether; and Paula, to whom this book is dedicated.

I want to remember some of my heavenly friends, in addition to the ones who come up in the stories that follow: Vicki Goldish, I still miss you; Rev. Sandy Taylor; Rev. Jim Harris; Dr. Gary McClelland; Edith Perry; Norm Mason; Rev. Jean White; Rev. Jean Hart; and hundreds of others. Dr. John Boswell, whose brilliance can never be replaced—what a model of courageous gay scholarship! Thank you Rev. Danny Mahoney, assistant pastor extraordinaire, who on your deathbed told me to finish the book. Thanks to Patrick, who stuck around only long enough to take care of Danny. Thank you, God, finally, for my dear father Ralph, whose laughter, love, and playfulness are such a blessed memory, and for my brother Dave, also gone too soon.

Thank you, finally, to all the people of Metropolitan Community Churches worldwide for your courage and faithfulness.

Introduction: Tribal Tales

Theologically speaking, I'm trying on the label *queer millennialist.* Theological labels and categories both confine and expand our thinking. "Queer millennialist" sounds both playful and radical.

I'll start by telling a sweet queer story. I began my life in the Metropolitan Community Churches (MCC) as a pastor in the oldest publicly queer denomination in the United States (and perhaps the world). Rob and I had been working on a community project—the third monument in the world to honor gay and lesbian protest. It was to memorialize several actions that had taken place on the Crescent Heights Triangle in West Hollywood, the most recent of which was the beginning of two solid weeks of nonviolent protests against Governor Pete Wilson's vetoing of the gay and lesbian rights bill, AB101. Rob and I went to a popular new gay coffee shop in West Hollywood, and Rob finally popped *the* question: "How can you be a Christian? You seem like a really great person." Rob was a thirtyish, wide-eyed activist still struggling with addiction recovery issues and in love with queer politics (most of the time). He was a very tall, handsome, fair-haired, beach-boy type who still had traces of adolescent gangliness.

I tried to account for myself. I tried not to be defensive about the church's wretched record of sexism, racism, and homophobia. I saw the look in his eyes, and I realized there were other questions to be asked. I asked, "Did you grow up in church?"

Rob flushed. Then he grinned, saying, "Yeah, I grew up going to a Lutheran parochial school."

"So," I said, "when did it happen? When did they break your heart?"

Bingo. He had that "How did you know?" look on his face. I find that, for many gay and lesbian people, *it* happened long before they knew they were queer. "Oh, yeah," Rob said, "there was the Jack Benny thing."

The Jack Benny thing? At six, Rob had taken piano lessons from a Lutheran church school teacher. While on his way to his piano lesson one day, he heard the news that Jack Benny had just died. Rob loved Jack Benny. I immediately understood. As a child, I had loved the comics and impersonators the best. There was Jack Benny, effeminate violin player, making fun of himself for our enjoyment. People admired and loved Jack Benny, and, as queer as it may sound, he made Rob feel safer in the world. I know he made me feel safer, too. Full of grief and questions, Rob asked his piano teacher, "Will Jack Benny go to heaven?"

"No," came the clear-cut answer. No, no, he was not Christian, or Lutheran, or *something*. So Rob learned that God didn't love Jack Benny—or at least that Lutherans didn't believe that God loved Jack Benny.

Rob's heart asked, "How can I love someone or something that God doesn't love enough to take into heaven? Or that God even hates?" Everything shattered in Rob's very tender and new life of faith. And it never got put back together again, at least not in the church.

It seems an incomprehensible cruelty: heaven without Jack Benny. A heaven without comedy or effeminate men—who wants to go there? An exclusive, hard-nosed God—the God who made Jack Benny, who could, with his eyes, the flick of a wrist, the perfect timing, make the world laugh—that same God wouldn't take Jack in? *What's wrong with this picture?* Just telling the story was painful for Rob. At first he thought it was silly. But then it became clear. *The Jack Benny thing* was Rob's first clue that the church that had raised him taught of a God who might not really love him after all. If God didn't want Jack Benny, what chance would Rob have? And how could he appeal this decision? So Rob left the Lutherans to their heaven without Jack Benny.

I told Rob that it was just possible that what he had really rejected was not God and maybe not even Christianity but a very tragic interpretation of both. I saw the spark of hope in Rob's eyes.

Rob ducked in and out of MCC for the next two years, full of queer ambivalence. Before he died of AIDS, he called me from his hospital bed with a great sermon idea for me about somebody he remembered from his Lutheran Sunday school days, a guy named Job. "I think Job was refusing to be a victim!" Rob declared. "Like me—why don't you preach about that?"

We tend to personalize Job, but Job's story is the devastating story of humanity and our planet. Mass murders in grade schools, in movie theaters, and in our streets, as well as wars with suicide bombers, drones, and black ops, are the modern-day trials of Job.

So just what in the world is going on? I think we are having a violent reaction of rage and helplessness because of the destabilization of nations and economies. Overpopulation, poverty, and hunger have not been improved by sweeping technological advances. We are all just more acutely aware of human needs. There is much debate about whether or not we are simply polluting and poisoning ourselves to death. Some say the environmentalists are a bunch of fanatics who don't appreciate the resiliency of nature. But the increasing toxicity of the environment cannot be ignored. We are sickened and dying from our polluted world.

In such a toxic environment, the poor, the minorities, and the politically vulnerable populations will be the first to exhibit signs and symptoms of the deteriorating immunological picture. It is the canary-in-the-mines syndrome. When miners wanted to know if a particular mine shaft was safe from poison gases, they sent in a canary first. If the canary returned, the miners felt safe to go in. On our planet today, poor people, people of color, women and children, and gays and lesbians are the canaries (or sitting ducks, if you prefer). Those who have any kind of privilege (gender, race, class, sexuality, or age) are better able, for a time, to buffer and insulate themselves from the toxic environment—from AIDS, cancer, and other diseases, for example—but not forever.

There is also an increasing moral and religious toxicity in reaction to so much social upheaval and change, as well as worldwide political challenges. This phenomenon is called in many religions *fundamentalism*. In a century of increasing engagement with diverse values, morality, and religions, fundamentalism provides absolutes and targets "enemies."

What does it mean to be a gay, lesbian, bisexual, or transgender person in this age of rage and reaction? It was the poet Judy Grahn who first spoke powerfully to me about an anthropology or sociology of what she calls transpeople (a broad category including gay, lesbian, transgender, and gender non-conforming people). For a long time, I have believed that theological anthropology (in the old days, this was called the "doctrine of man") was the church's major problem in acceptance of gay, lesbian, bisexual, and transgender people. Because of this nonacceptance, we are a kind of people—sexual minorities through no choice of our own.

It was only in the middle of the last century that gays and lesbians began to ask the question about the *"love that dare not speak its name."* But they did not dare to theologize much about this love—or even to philosophize much—until later decades.

Gender non-conforming people finally had practical medical options in the 1950s and are challenging a simplistic understanding of binary biology and theology.

Biblical theology must account for tribal structures—groups of people who are bound by blood, culture, religion, laws, and mutual understanding. In the 20th century, gay and trans subcultures provided privacy and social opportunities that felt like tribal bonds, with code words, networks, and a sense of both shared danger and safe spaces.

So, does identification with our "tribe" or sub-culture give us the courage and strength to claim our humanness? Or does it urge us to compare ourselves, to judge ourselves as worse or better than others? Dominant culture wants the rest of us to focus on our generic humanness, on how alike we are, and not on our differences. Is the notion of generic humanness essentially classist, racist, sexist?[1] Michelle Alexander's book title, *The New Jim Crow: Mass Incarceration in the Age of Colorblindness* (New Press, 2012) is a powerful reminder that, just because we don't want to see oppression, it doesn't mean that the impact is not real.

Only 42 years ago, Rev. Troy Perry wrote an open letter to the church in his book, *The Lord Is My Shepherd and He [sic] Knows I'm Gay*: "I am not a creature from the other darkness, I am a man of flesh and blood."[2] In many places in the world and still in this country, it is our humanness as gays and lesbians that is still the issue.

I met Kiron (not his real name), a gay East Indian man, the way I meet many people these days. His partner, Jerry, was dying of AIDS. Jerry's parents stayed in Kiron and Jerry's home in Los Angeles during Jerry's final days. Jerry's mother, in fact, lived there for months. Kiron cared for Jerry until he had to go to the hospital. Jerry's parents were never openly rude to Kiron, but he knew they had never approved of Jerry's life. Nevertheless, Kiron showed them every kindness, gave them a key to his home, and was very hospitable. The day after Jerry died, Kiron went to work in his law office as usual. He was not out to his colleagues or clerical staff and felt he could not risk being absent from work, *even the day after his partner of six years had died.*

When he returned home that night, the apartment felt strange. Then he realized that Jerry's parents had left and had taken many things—all of Jerry's possessions and things that belonged to both of them, including precious photographs and personal effects. Kiron collapsed in grief and rage. In order for these good, churchgoing folks to do such a thing, they had to be willing to see Kiron as less than human, not deserving of ordinary human courtesy and respect, much less gratitude. They had to be willing to negate all the evidence of the love and commitment between their son and this gentle, good man. Kiron never saw Jerry's parents or any of his things again.[3]

When people are treated as undeserving of basic human respect and dignity, we turn away and turn to each other. Tribal boundaries and identities are a matter of survival. When we find each other, we want to stand back-to-back to defend each other, but we belong to a network of tribes and identities. In church "tribes," survival—jobs, families, friends—still often depend on "discretion" and secrecy.

Secrecy was the rule when I met Chris Cowap in 1974 at the first meeting of the NCC's Commission on Women in Ministry. It was an incredible gathering of about 120 powerful women church leaders and feminists. My invitation was a last-minute one, thanks to Roy Birchard, pastor of Metropolitan Community Church of New York, who doubled as a secretary for the Presbyterians at the "God Box" (a term of affection for the Inter-Church Center at 475 Riverside Drive in Manhattan). I got a *gay underground* invitation, which meant that I would never know precisely how I got invited.

I was 23 at the time and still at MCC Boston, and I was the only *out* lesbian at this meeting. Just by showing up, I evidently caused quite a stir, and people went out of their way to either greet me or avoid me. By the end of the weekend, after dozens of midnight tearful conversations and hallway comings-out, I'd guess that nearly one-third of those women were lesbians or bisexual. It was an exhilarating and exhausting introduction to the world of ecumenical feminism of the Seventies.

But, of all of them, Chris probably affected me the most. An intense, politically savvy lay Episcopalian and career social-justice ecumenist, Chris was already an instant hero to me. When she wanted to speak to me, I was flattered and curious. She just looked at me, shook her head, and said tearfully, "I'm just never going to be able to do it."

"Do what?" I asked. (Duh!)

"Come out, like you." Chris was a lesbian! Well, of course. She just kept shaking her head. She told me about her activism in the civil rights movement, her feminist identification, her commitment to progressive environmental causes and to human rights. But, she said, "I can't do this last thing. I can't do this last thing that is really for and about me. And I'm ashamed. When I look at you, I'm ashamed. I'm ashamed I can't do it for myself and that I can't be more supportive of you." I remember just holding her a while and thanking her for coming out to me. I tried to reassure her that I did feel supported, just by her human example.

From time to time after that, whenever I was in New York, I would try to find Chris, while minimizing the danger of exposing her. She moved around in the God Box quite a bit, first to the World Council of Churches (WCC) and then later back to the National Council of Churches (NCC). I remember sneaking up to her office with Rev. Karen Ziegler, trying to be invisible on the way! ("Nah, I didn't just see two lesbians sneaking by into Chris's office, did you?") Chris always looked glad to see me, and the feeling was mutual. Plus, she possessed a wealth of knowledge about everything ecumenical. She was my inside track.

Through the ecumenical feminist grapevine, I eventually heard about her lung cancer. When we applied for membership in the NCC in 1981, Chris had just gone into remission and was coming back to work. Seeing her at those meetings was wonderful. She provided great support to us in those days—and eventually around to the AIDS issue.

In early November 1983, I stopped at my brother's home in Indianapolis. I was on the way to the Hartford meeting of the NCC, during which they would be voting on our eligibility for membership. Chris tracked me down in Indianapolis—Chris often managed to track me down. I liked that and had always attributed a certain omniscience to her, and this only reinforced it. She opened with "I'm gonna do it!"

"Do what?" (Duh, again.)

"Come out." She said she figured there had to be a reason for all this cancer remission stuff. And this must be it. (Chris always skipped formalities in conversations with me. She talked as if we had spoken just yesterday and not six months before.) She told me that, if the NCC turned MCC down for eligibility or membership, she would publicly come out at the meeting in Hartford. All I could think of was our first meeting and how

Chris thought she could never do it. She had been a person for all people but not quite a person for herself. And perhaps now that was about to change. No longer a generic person, Chris could claim her lesbian self.

The Hartford NCC meeting was a zoo. The *Inclusive Language Lectionary* was being introduced. Virginia Mollenkott, a member of the committee, infuriated some of her colleagues by coming out at that meeting in support of MCC. The Lectionary Committee had excited so much attention from the press and religious conservatives that our issue seemed overshadowed at times. The committee had, in fact, been subjected to harassing phone calls and even death threats that had necessitated calling in the FBI. The NCC received much more negative mail about the lectionary than it *ever* received about the MCC. They still published the lectionary, which many of us in MCC use—but they rejected MCC.

After days of ecu-political machinations, the die was cast. A poorly written "compromise" motion was adopted by the NCC that would *postpone indefinitely* their vote on our eligibility for membership.

They couldn't say yes, but they couldn't say no either. (This would become something of a dysfunctional pattern in the MCC/NCC relationship, the "come here/go away" version of ecu-teasing.) It was as if they said, "We can't bear to think of ourselves as rejecting you, so we'll just call it something else and keep everyone guessing." Except the cynics, of course, who knew all along.

When the vote happened, I was immediately called out into the hallway in front of 50 or 60 reporters, TV cameras, microphones, and so on to read our prepared statement, putting a cautiously optimistic spin on it all. We queers were good sports in those days.

Meanwhile, Chris sat in her seat, a little numb and confused. She had a prearranged signal with Dr. Jane Carey Peck, professor of ethics at Andover Newton School of Theology and on the United Methodist delegation to the governing board of the NCC. If the vote was negative, Chris would stand, and Jane Carey would look for her and yield the floor to her. (As a member of the staff, Chris did not automatically have a voice at the governing board meeting.) The only problem was that, when the vote happened, Chris was not sure just *how* negative it was, and she sat there, trying to decide. Then, as she told Virginia Mollenkott and me later that evening, she suddenly felt two hands on her shoulders lifting her out of her seat. When she turned around to see who had done it, no one was there.

Jane Carey got the signal and yielded the floor to Chris. The room was utterly still. Someone came running out into the hallway to get me, saying, "Chris is at the mic!" I got into the meeting room in time to hear this:

DR. JANE CAREY PECK: Jane Carey Peck, United Methodist. I ask for a point of personal privilege in order to yield the floor to a staff member of the Division of Church and Society, one of the valued and leading contributors to our common work, Chris Cowap.

CHRIS COWAP: I don't want to be here. And I don't have any choice. Dr. Lois Wilson said this morning that "to be a person is to be relational; that's what defines us." I want to define myself in her terms.

I am a daughter; I am a sister; I am an aunt; I'm a friend; I'm a colleague; for almost ten years now I've been a servant in this community of the council; and I'm a woman who loves another woman. And I'm sure with every fiber of my being that I am a child of God and an inheritor of the kingdom of heaven. When I have felt God's judgment on me—and I have, too many times—it has never been because of the nature of those relationships. It's been because I have allowed them or caused them to be broken, to be not-love.

I said I don't want to be here—right here—and yet I feel compelled right now by the Holy Spirit to be here, saying this. I hear this: not a heavenly choir but a single voice, singing 'Hodie! This is the day, Chris, when you must, in love, assert in this community in which you have been called to serve, to these brothers and sisters in Christ with whom you have been in community, you must affirm God's affirmation of you. You can't do anything else.' This has not simply been an institutional matter, and you know that I am not speaking as one lone individual. I'm not speaking as a spokesperson; I wasn't chosen as a spokesperson. But you know that there are other people in this room—in the choir lofts, in the sacristies, in the pews, in the seminaries, in your national staffs—for whom I am speaking. I believe that you honestly intend, some of you, to continue in the dialogue and to wrestle with prayer and continued pain with the questions of what it means to be human and what it means to be truly members of one another. And you need to know that there are some of us who feel called by God to be here and to stay here to be in that kind of dialogue with you.[4]

Chris Cowap died four and a half years later of lung cancer. In her final years, I had the privilege of rooming with Chris several times at NCC meetings. We never talked about it (she was always businesslike), so I don't know which of us got the bigger kick out of watching people trying not to wonder just what was "going on." Mostly what was going on was that Chris would regale me (and sometimes Sandi Robinson, president of MCC's Samaritan College) with wonderful feminist ecumenical folklore. She especially loved to tell Claire Randall stories. While drinking her white wine, Chris (who was mostly bald from chemo-therapy) would take off her wig and NCC drag, don a comfortable white T-shirt, and talk, and talk, and talk.

And sometimes we touched. Like the time she was in such excruciating pain (from the progressing cancer) that I had her lie on her side while I laid hands on her chest and back, doing light massage and heavy prayer.

Chris eventually succumbed, but not before she had resolved in herself that terrible tension between her commitment to all people and all the earth and her commitment to her own special and lovely tribe. When *they* put their hands on her that afternoon in Hartford, lifting her out of her seat, they helped her to do what had seemed so remote and utterly impossible only nine years before.

In many ways, the ecumenical movement is the only other "church" I've ever felt completely at home in besides MCC. It has been a source of some of my most powerful spiritual experiences and deepest friendships.

In 1991, I had the privilege of serving as MCC's delegate observer to the World Council of Churches General Assembly in Canberra, Australia. The first Sunday we were there, we shared the very first celebration of the "Lima Liturgy"[5] at a WCC assembly. This was the first chance for this world ecumenical assembly to celebrate communion with the carefully crafted and negotiated words. Even the Eastern Orthodox agreed on the wording of the liturgy. The only barrier was that they, and some others, could still not agree on who was legitimately able to preside over communion. So it was still far from perfect, and incomplete as an ecumenical Eucharist. Nevertheless, the celebration went forward that day, with 5,000 or so in attendance under that big, open tent under the big, open Australian summer sky. Outside, conservative Eastern Orthodox people protested the celebration, criticizing Orthodox ecumenists with huge, vilifying signs. I think some fundamentalist critics were there, too.

The liturgy was breathtakingly gorgeous. Aboriginal participation hallowed the ground and space; the processional was grand. A young, tall, adorable lesbian with a buzz haircut towered above the others. I noticed her right away. Steve Pieters, Kit Cherry, and I poked each other with the "We are everywhere!" poke.

Then came the invitation to communion, and people began to do just as we do in MCC, to stream forward down the aisle, mostly single file, to receive the holy elements. Other than Kit and Steve, I knew no one else in our section of the tent. I probably knew only about 200 of the 5,000 people there that day. Suddenly, I was overwhelmed. I saw the faces of hundreds and hundreds of strangers streaming down the aisles, hungry and thirsty, with hardly a dry eye. We were all aware of the beauty and pain and historicity of this moment. And then it seemed to me that I actually *knew* all of these strangers. They looked just like people I served communion to every Sunday at MCC Los Angeles. Well, not *just* like, but very close.

They were all races, nations, sizes, shapes, sexualities, and ages. I am always amazed at what happens to tired, older, dry, craggy adult faces when they come to communion. How faces soften, open, even glow. How older people start to look younger. Wide-eyed, open, trusting, needy, and unashamed—it was as if I knew every person who streamed forward. Suddenly, it was as if I could have told you, if you had asked me, not only every name but every story, their fears, dreams, how they "got over" (a Mahalia Jackson song), how they got there. I began to cry, something I did very infrequently in those days. I remembered Søren Kierkegaard's words to the effect that if we knew *everything* about a person—their pain, fears, losses, loves—we could not help but love them to death.

Suddenly, proud to be representing my tribe, I was transported to a post-tribal reality. It no longer mattered; everything was dissolving, especially me. Never in all my life had I experienced the sense of overpowering connectedness to the earth and all her people. And then it shifted just a little bit more. I was a child in a huge family gathering. Somehow along the way I had lost contact with my parents, which was very frightening. But there was this deep consolation, because all the folks around me had this vague *family resemblance* that made me feel safe, at home. Just like the ways my Aunt Betty and Aunt Jo looked enough like my mom so that just seeing them always made me feel secure, like it would all be okay somehow. If I lost my parents, my family, my tribal connections of whatever type, I was still safe in the arms of this extended tribal network. Now my tears were of belonging and relief.

I'm not sure how long that experience lasted. Eventually, I got up and made my way forward to the most ecumenical Eucharist the world had experienced to date. I joined my gay and lesbian tribe to partake with the rest—One Body, One Blood.

1 • Healing Our Tribal Wounds

The religious right in the United States (now often called the "religious wrong" by some) is fond of going on and on about a *gay agenda*. It has become clear over the years that our agenda is dignity, fairness, and equality. But, beyond that, I believe that we need a tribal agenda with two urgent components: *healing our tribal wounds* and *boldly exercising our tribal gifts*.

When "Don't Ask, Don't Tell" was repealed, I remembered the whole process going back to the Clinton years. Lifting the ban on gays and lesbians in the military was not really at the top of the charts in terms of the agenda for the gay and lesbian organizations of that time. A lot of the gay and lesbian movement leaders were boomers, some of whom were antiwar activists in the Sixties and Seventies, and they were not willing to portray gays and lesbians as pro-military or patriotic. Yet history and circumstances pushed this issue to the top when Bill Clinton was elected president. There are huge numbers of gay and lesbian veterans—and gays and lesbians currently serving with honor. Something about the psychology and sociology of minority group legitimacy in the American mind is related to military status. Pragmatically, the military can be a stepping stone out of poverty. Symbolically, it seems to be the test of "true citizenship," which in political currency is the *same thing* as "humanness."

This came home to me at the funeral of an older African-American gay clergyman who had been on the staff of MCC Los Angeles for several years. Thomas Walker was a gentle, beloved man who had devoted his ministry to helping alcoholics like himself. I do not remember knowing before his death that Thomas was also a U.S. Navy veteran.

I presided over his funeral, which was attended by many of his family, by their Baptist pastor, and by many MCC people and members of Alcoholics Anonymous. Thomas, in his death, had assembled a very eclectic group. As we bid him farewell at the end of the funeral, and after the last "Amen," the director of the funeral home, as is customary at the funerals of veterans, gave an American flag to the family. We were gathered in the lower level of the mausoleum in which Thomas was being buried. I had forgotten about this final bit of funeral procedure. As the funeral director took the flag to present it to Thomas's brother, he said something like, "On behalf of the president of the United States, a grateful nation presents this flag to you."

Grief cracked open like a huge egg, at least for the MCC folks. I thought about how many times I had been at the funerals of veterans. The words had always seemed like an afterthought, even an intrusion. But context is everything. This time, the context was history itself. Only a few months before, a new president of the United States had actually uttered aloud the words "gay and lesbian" for the very first time and had, at great political cost to himself, declared his belief that we were citizens, human beings, and worthy of military status (in other words, human dignity and rights). If he never did another thing, the fact that he did that for us was an incredible, costly gift. So, when this funeral director said those words at the funeral of a black gay veteran, it all just came together. We just wept as he said, "On behalf of the president"— Bill Clinton, who could at least say the words "gay and lesbian"—"a grateful nation." Imagine it. The United States expressed its gratitude for *our* Thomas.

Comparisons of oppression are at times very odious to me. But the *feeling* in that room reminded me of the feelings I saw in another room just weeks later, at the conclusion of the federal trial of the four officers accused of violating the civil rights of Rodney King. The picture of the sanctuary of First AME Church in Los Angeles comes to mind, and the tears of relief and joy. And Jesse Jackson wiping away his own tears, saying, "It's just so hard to have to go through all this drama to get simple justice." Nothing in that whole day touched me more than that comment. The joy and bitterness commingled. Out of these battles, we gleaned meaning, but all the problems still remain. The war goes on.

It's just so hard to have to go through all this drama for some simple justice. Just to be considered human, worthy of citizenship, worthy of heaven.

Justice in heaven and on earth is the stuff of queer millennialist theology. In times of slavery and its aftermath, the question about black people's souls, about that dimension and percentages of their humanness, was dehumanizing. But eventually it almost seemed as if heaven, for blacks, and in fact for all poor people, was viewed as a consolation prize for having no justice on earth.

For gays and lesbians, it's a little different. Being able to be closeted means that gays and lesbians have been able to pass and use race, gender, or class privilege, where possible, to get the goodies here on earth. The stereotype of the gay and lesbian political establishment as a white, wealthy minority who can push our agenda has often been accurate. Poor, working-class, and nonwhite lesbian, gay, bisexual, and transgender (LGBT) people have too often been shunted aside. Lesbians are disproportionately represented in every women's prison I've ever visited, and these were not lesbians who were only lesbian during their prison sentence. Transgender people are targeted for violence and more so if they are persons of color.

All hell broke loose when U.S. Representative Barney Frank teamed up with the Human Rights Campaign to remove "gender identity" from the Employment Non-Discrimination Act (ENDA). The thought was akin to dispensationalist Christianity—that salvation comes in waves. It was a move parallel to the series of decisions on voting rights—white women were pitted against black men with an underlying belief that the world couldn't handle both. So African-American men received the vote, then later all women gained suffrage. The earthly stuff of voting and jobs are usually framed in the ethereal stuff of heaven.

Queer millennialist theology is about justice that begins on earth but must include heaven. It is tempting for us to ignore ideas about an afterlife because the issue of heaven has been really touchy for gays and lesbians. It's the "Jack Benny thing." So I make it my practice to talk about heaven casually, freely, and frequently, as if with Emily Dickinson:

> I never saw a moor,
> I never saw the sea;
> Yet know I how the heather looks,
> And what a wave must be.
>
> I never spoke with God,
> Nor visited in heaven;
> Yet certain am I of the spot
> As if the chart were given.[6]

"The chart was given," and I am familiar with "the spot." Of course we're all going to get there. *And I won't go without you.*

Once, while debating Jerry Falwell on Ron Reagan Jr.'s television show, I got to deliver one of my favorite "gays goin' to heaven" sound bites. I said, "Jerry, the only reason I would want to die before you is that I want to be on heaven's welcome wagon and see the look on your face when you get there." He actually chuckled, turned to me at the break, and said, "That was very good!"

When the National Council of Churches of Christ voted in the fall of 1992 to *take no action* on our request for observer status (as if that in itself were not an action!), I managed to be able to say how grateful I was for MCC because it was there that I learned that, thank God, "it was easier to get into heaven than into the National Council of Churches of Christ in the U.S.A.!" That little *sound bite* made it to newspapers in Holland, Hong Kong, and around the world. I liked saying it because it assumes that gay and lesbian people are eligible for heaven. That assumption is contained in the grammar of the sentence. And when I speak about God or heaven, I always want gay men and lesbians to hear the assumption of our eligibility (for heaven, if not for the NCC).

Healing Wounds of False Witness

What are the wounds of our people—the gay, lesbian, bisexual, and transgender communities and tribes?

Clearly, rejection and abandonment are at the top of the list—rejection and abandonment by our families, churches, synagogues, and governments. But also high on the list for me is the damage caused by *slander.* There is no explicit condemnation of homosexuality among the Ten Commandments in the Bible, but there *is* a commandment against *bearing false witness against your neighbor.* Virginia Mollenkott and Letha Scanzoni wrote a book with the wonderful title *Is the Homosexual My Neighbor?* If the answer to that rhetorical question is yes, then the assumption must be that gay and lesbian people are human, are our neighbors, and that it displeases God if we tell lies about them! The Bible doesn't seem to say whether it's worse if the lies are told out of malice or ignorance. False witness is false witness.

The fact is that the *radical* or *religious* right breaks the Ninth Commandment every day, using ignorance and fear of homosexuality and homosexuals to raise millions and millions of dollars. But they are not alone. The whole church and other religious bodies have borne false witness about gays and lesbians for hundreds and maybe thousands of years.

One of the most painful false negative stereotypes about gay and lesbian people is that we are child molesters. For many, many years, police statistics have demonstrated that the vast majority (more than 90 percent) of child molesters are heterosexual men. There is no factual basis whatsoever for the belief that gay men or lesbians are any more likely than heterosexuals to seduce or molest children or adolescents. Yet this fear and false witness are kept alive in the popular mind.

In Uganda, the perennial "anti-homosexuality" bill is largely based on the long debunked myth that gay people "recruit" minors and sexually abuse them to make them gay. It is ironic—and tragic—that fundamentalist evangelists from the United States have helped perpetrate these lies, even as they are losing credibility in the United States.

This false witness has stigmatized our love and our families and is one of several factors contributing to irrational, fevered-pitch homophobia. Sadly, gays and lesbians must heal from our internalized response to this stigma. One of our responses has been to be afraid of children and of interacting with them to avoid any possible cause for the accusation of child molestation. I remember, particularly in the Seventies, this came out as a thinly veiled hostility toward children when we called straight people *breeders* and referred to their children as *rug rats*. There was the occasional lesbian mother who still had custody of her children, and a very rare father or two.

Underneath that defensive posture always lurked the deep-seated fear, "What if *they* are right?" Are children really safe with us? When I became the Pastor of MCC Detroit in 1975, the church had a *policy* that no one under the age of 18 could attend MCC without being accompanied by a parent or guardian. I was stunned that a church would feel it was too risky to welcome unaccompanied minors. This was both a fear of the false accusations that could be made *and* a deep-seated uneasiness that maybe children weren't really safe with us. And that was simply internalized homophobia. I told them I would not pastor a church in which children were not safe or welcome. And in any case, we couldn't keep them away. The children managed to find us on their own.

Roger was 13 when he came to MCC Detroit. He knew he was gay, and he was very mature-appearing for his age, as well as sexually precocious. He often managed to get into gay bars and was constantly harassed at school. He was working "the block" (every city has a gay cruising area where closeted gay or bisexual men pick up hustlers or street kids for quick sex). An extremely closeted member of my church picked Roger up, then realized how old he was. The member called me in a panic. He brought Roger to me at the church office and dropped him off. I called his mother. She couldn't handle him, and I, in fact, got written permission from her for him to attend the church. Two adult men in the church took Roger under their wings. These were two men who did not exploit him sexually but gave him support and sometimes even shelter. They did this at great risk to themselves. We managed to help get Roger safely through junior high, and he eventually moved to San Francisco to complete high school.

Metropolitan Community Church of Los Angeles tells the story of a young boy (not older than 12), a runaway, who appeared on the steps of the church on a Sunday in the early Seventies. He wanted to go home. So the assistant pastor took him to the police. It is hard for anyone who is not gay or lesbian and over 35 to understand what an enormous act of courage this was on the part of the pastor. The pastor explained what had happened, and the police spent time interrogating the boy, trying to find out, among other things, if these homosexuals had molested him in any way. Finally, one of the officers said, "Son, do you know what kind of church this is?"

The boy thought for a minute and replied, "I don't know. I guess it's just a church for everybody." That story has been told a lot at MCC Los Angeles. It contains a lot of healing messages.

MCC says we are a church for everybody—even children. In the 1980s, two things happened, it almost seems simultaneously: the AIDS epidemic and a baby boom. More lesbians and gay men were fighting for the right to have full or partial custody of their children from heterosexual marriages or relationships. And lesbians were seeking other ways to have children, especially through artificial insemination and adoption. Some gay men also donated sperm or sought to adopt.

Many MCC churches now have child care or children's programs. By the turn of the millennium, it was coined the "gayby boom." But we were still fighting the remnants of the negative power of false witness. Even in the midst of efforts to defeat Prop 8 in California, movement strategists refused to put LGBT people and their children in the public light because focus groups said voters in focus groups reacted negatively. In the recent successful marriage equality campaigns in Washington, Minneapolis, Maryland, and Maine, LGBT families and their children began to be featured—although the straight allies have sometimes supplanted LGBT people in campaign ads. In the burgeoning sex scandals connected to the Vatican, efforts still emerge to blame gay priests—although media have generally been well-informed about the facts that pedophilia is overwhelmingly a heterosexual problem.

I have come to believe that our capacity to welcome children into our gay and lesbian families, organizations, churches, and so on is one measure of how much healing we have experienced. Our resistance to children is our resistance to our own healing. The safer children are with us, the safer we are with ourselves and each other.

More often than not, our gay or lesbian inner child was rejected, abandoned, or abused. I believe that oftentimes our families knew before we did that we were gay or lesbian. At least that we were *different—they* may not have known why. But we were different, some of us "passing" for straight better than others. And that difference was *not* perceived as a good thing. It caused us to be punished, humiliated, and targeted for abuse.

It has not been easy for gay men and lesbians to admit these childhood wounds, partly because of another false witness. That one said that we *became* gay or lesbian because of an "absent father" and an "overbearing mother"; or because we were molested by an older homosexual (and then wanted to grow up and be one?); or molested heterosexually (and we hated it and wanted *not* to be one of them?). To admit to having been targeted for emotional or physical abuse seemed to be contributing to a negative stereotype! So many of us were anxious—in fact, overanxious—to prove that we came from "normal" homes and parents, which most of us did. Today, we know that too many "normal homes and parents" in the United States are violent and abusive—something we came to know through research—and truth telling.

If you read Troy Perry's two books, separated by nearly two decades, you can see the difference. In *The Lord Is My Shepherd and He [sic] Knows I'm Gay*, Troy presents a mostly happy childhood picture, glossing over some crucial issues. In *Don't Be Afraid Anymore*, he tells some terrible stories about violence in his family and childhood. It became safer and more acceptable for Troy to tell those stories in the late 1980s.

And telling those stories is what we must do if we are to heal and if we are really to be a safe haven for the children we want to welcome into our lives.

I met Rechal in October 1985. She was three years old, and I met her in prison.

She and her mother were in prison together in a special facility operated by the California Correctional System. This program and several others like it probably had good theory and intentions. It was a locked facility for women who had infants or toddlers. The theory was that these women and their children would benefit from not losing contact with one another during the crucial formative years. Also, the women could be given assistance in learning parenting skills.

Instead, this program, in my opinion, amounted to women in prison providing the care for these children for free, so that the state would not have to pay for their support while the mothers were in prison—a budget-cutting reform. I observed no classes or other assistance in parenting skills. And because these women were locked up 24 hours a day, they had 24-hour sole care of the children, with no breaks provided.

Jessie was an attractive 38-year old career criminal and the mother of Rechal (by artificial insemination). Jessie had been introduced to the Mexican equivalent of the Mafia at an early age by her family. She laundered money and did robberies. She was openly proud of the fact that she had refused to engage in prostitution and had always lived her lesbian identity. She had been party to a killing, something she could never bring herself to talk about with me.

As happens with organized crime, Jessie had ended up owing someone a lot of money (she was a heroin addict). Rechal was a late-in-life baby that she desperately wanted to have, and she finally really wanted to get off drugs and out of the organized crime scene. So she agreed to assist in *one last* diamond heist to pay off her debt. She was arrested, and Rechal was taken from her.

While in prison, Jessie heard of MCC. When she got released to this special facility for mothers and their children, she contacted me at MCC's headquarters. She had called other gay and lesbian organizations looking for support or help—to no avail. MCC Los Angeles had just begun an outreach program at California Institute for Women, and Jessie's partner, Carol, gave her our phone number.

Jessie was shocked when someone actually called her back. I asked her if she wanted me to come visit her. She was cautious, but said yes. A few days later I showed up, wearing my clerical collar, at the facility (which was temporarily housed in one wing of a rehab center in South Central Los Angeles).

After I cleared security, they let me in the locked ward. Jessie and Rechal greeted me. I picked up three-year-old Rechal and fell in love at first sight. She sat on my lap, pointed to my collar, and said, "Jesus?" Then she asked me if I was a boy or a girl (Rechal had only been to Catholic churches at this point in her life). After we established my name and gender, I got to know them both—over several months.

Jessie asked me to baptize Rechal and to become her godmother. It was clear that Jessie had few friends and resources that she could count on, and her family was simply not an option. Jessie began testing me. Was I reliable? In retrospect, I know she was trying to determine if her child would be safe with me.

After many long months, after taking care of Rechal for three weeks while Jessie recovered from surgery in the institution, I helped find a housing situation for Jessie and Rechal with the plan that they would receive support and help from the MCC community.

It seemed ideal. My friend Judi had an adopted son and a large home. We worked on the finances and the roommate arrangement, and I began talking with Jessie about what she really wanted in her life. She was a jazz pianist, and she was going to play in church sometime soon. She had been off drugs since before Rechal was born. It seemed very hopeful to me.

One week after their release from prison, Jessie died of a heroin overdose in the bathroom of my friend's home. Rechal was with her for four hours, curled up beside her, before Judi and her son came home and found them.

The next week was a nightmare of waiting to find out about Rechal's whereabouts. The police had taken her into protective custody and would not let me take her home with me. Judi and I spent days talking about what was best for Rechal. Judi had a lot of experience with children who had been traumatized. We came to the conclusion that, if Judi could adopt her, I could continue to be in Rechal's life as an "extra mommy"—that is, godmother.

Miraculously, in March of 1986, an L.A. court agreed. When Re-chal's grandmother decided to try to get involved, an independent, court-appointed guardian investigated. It was Rechal's grandmother who had gotten Jessie involved in organized crime and probably with drugs. The court believed us, and Rechal now has a home and a wonderful, large family that includes other abandoned, endangered children.

Rechal is one of thousands and thousands of children who have been lucky enough to find safe, loving, gay and lesbian homes to live in. Gay men and lesbians were among the first people to offer foster care and adoption to children with HIV and AIDS. When others were afraid, gay men and lesbians, who already had had lots of contact with people with AIDS, were not afraid to touch or love these children. Lesbians founded most of the agencies that service children with HIV and AIDS. The wounds from the false witness of church and society against us will take a long time to heal, especially the insinuation that we are gay or lesbian because of a poor upbringing, and that we are all consequently child molesters. Only telling the stories of the healing of our own families of origin from this false witness, and the creation of our own families of choice (which often include children), will begin to heal these wounds completely.

The Wounds From Projection And Repression

I think the other way in which gay and lesbian people and other sexual minorities experience oppression is that we have endured the massive projection of society's sexual fears and fantasies.

Most minorities experience sexual projection as part of their oppression. African Americans, male and female, experience sexual projection as part of the package of white racism. African-American men have been stereotyped as sexually obsessed and violent (there is, for example, the "myth of the black rapist"),[7] and African-American women have been stereotyped as promiscuous. Asian Americans are considered sexually exotic by the white majority, and Latins are supposed to be "hot." And, of course, sexism's major features include the projection of male fears and fantasies onto women so that women are not real people but objects available for male sexual pleasure or objects over which men can exercise power and control.

If racial and ethnic minorities are the objects of sexual projection, how much more is this true for sexual minorities for which the issue of sexuality is already at the forefront of the debate?

Society's hatred and loathing of homosexuals is really about the collective shame, guilt, fear, and self-hatred in our culture at large, especially as these are related to issues of sexuality.

Presbyterians and Human Sexuality, published in 1991 by the Special Committee on Human Sexuality of the Presbyterian Church in the United States, is still perhaps the best and most comprehensive statement on human sexuality and ethical consideration. It states, "The special committee noticed how the problem of homosexuality is commonly used in our churches to refer indirectly to any and all forms of sexual nonconformity, whether among gay persons or non-gays. Homosexuality is typically invoked in a rhetorical, almost formulaic way to signal that something has gone wrong. However, homosexuality often remains an abstraction, unrelated to—and uninformed by—real people. It functions primarily as a powerful symbolic carrier of people's fears and discomfort about sexuality in general."[8]

I'm tempted to say here, "We knew that!" Gay and lesbian people, however, *do* and *do not* know this. Sometimes it comes out in the kind of campy, teasing, "gotcha" gay-pride rhetoric: "Two, four, six, eight, is your husband really straight?" "We are your worst fears and your best fantasies." "We are the people your mother warned you about." And so on!

At other times, we gays and lesbians are ourselves bewildered. In many ways, we are symbolic of the current struggle over changing sexual roles that is going on in many cultures. That struggle is occurring in the context of a global women's movement that seeks to expose and bring about the end of patriarchy. No wonder there is a lot of fear and projection going on.

I never feel like such an object of projection as I do when I am in a predominantly heterosexual setting, like at the NCC meetings. Just by showing up, I trigger people's questions, fears, anxieties, and fantasies about homosexuality or sexuality in general. This is exhausting. And yet it feels like it is part of my job to invite questions, speculations, *even* their projections. But I find myself wanting to retreat to the safety of my queer community.

It is one thing to experience the sometimes amusing yet sometimes insulting projections of ordinary, everyday, garden-variety homophobes. It is still another thing to be the projection of the church's or society's fears to the degree that one is labeled evil or demonic. This is another experience that ordinary gay and lesbian people have—some frequently, some from time to time. I know many gays and lesbians who have been forbidden to have any contact with their own children, nieces, or nephews because of the assumed "toxicity" of their presence or influence. Other gay, lesbian, or transgender people have been publicly outed, humiliated, vilified, and literally driven out of a church meeting or Bible study, or pastor's office, or confessional. Many people do not have the resources internally to cope with these experiences. Some do not understand that this is a result of homophobia. They really believe they must deserve it, even if they can't figure out why.

The other wound related to projection is that of repression. We become obsessed with what we repress. Our culture has historically been sexually repressive and has *become* sexually obsessive. The gay and lesbian movement is both a consequence of and a contributor to this progression from repression to obsession. If society has repressed homosexuals and homosexuality, then it is also likely to become obsessed with it. Just think of how often gays and lesbians have been the subject of talk shows. Talking about homosexuality almost assures a good audience. Televangelists know that by talking about us on television or in their fund-raising mail they will get a lot of attention and response. If both repression and obsession are unhealthy and damaging responses to the gift of human sexuality, than what *should* be happening?

That's the key, I think. Sexuality is a part of our humanness that needs to be accepted, nurtured, and valued as a gift. My friend, the Rev. Ed Bacon, pastor of All Saints Episcopal Church in Pasadena, California, was a guest on an Oprah special show about spirituality and assured a young gay male caller that "Being gay is a gift from God." Oprah received so many responses to this statement that she did a follow-up show on the topic.

Meanwhile, however, homosexuality does not *feel* like a gift to the dominant culture! It represents all the "bad" things that sex is: dirty, promiscuous, shameful, perverted, weird, unhealthy, predatory, bad for children, nonproductive.

Many heterosexual people imagine that gay sexuality *feels* perverted, weird, and slimy, even to us! As gay and lesbian children grow up, we learn, overtly or indirectly, how dirty and awful "it" is. Then come the conflicting thoughts, feelings, longings, and desires. How can I want to touch and be touched in a way that feels "bad" or that God and everyone else will hate?

I remember first knowing that there were gay men when I was in junior high school. The limited information I had was that they all lived in Greenwich Village, New York, or on Fire Island (off of Long Island, where I lived). What I understood was that they were men who wore dresses and acted effeminate. It was years before I knew that they actually had sex with each other.

As a budding teen, I learned the words *queer* and *lezzie*. A "lezzie" was a tomboy who forgot to grow out of it. I was a tomboy who was making a valiant effort to grow out of it. Lezzies wanted to be boys. I may have even known that lezzies wanted to touch other girls the ways boys were supposed to want to touch girls. Actually, I didn't know very much about that either, come to think of it. I knew the essentials about the mechanics of heterosexual intercourse. But my mother told me that you were only supposed to do this when you were married. She blushed when she told me. And she told me it was enjoyable. I remember having serious doubts about that at the time. I knew that my parents hugged and kissed—I saw them do it. And they certainly liked it. *I* liked being hugged and kissed. So they hugged and kissed, and then, at some opportune moment, he stuck his penis into her vagina. I did not even understand this as a *process*, only as an event! I did not understand *lovemaking* as an activity that would take some time. Only gradually, I suppose, as I saw peers "making out" or as movies became a little more graphic did I understand anything about heterosexual sexual arousal. So it was all very strange and mysterious. I was in seminary and 21 years old before I ever recall seeing an erect penis. It was an 80-year-old disabled priest's in the hospital where I worked. (He was on a powerful drug whose side effect was sexual arousal.) Every other penis I'd seen had been flaccid. Only then did I actually understand how the penis got into the vagina.

I do remember the night that my friend Jean came over to the house where I was baby-sitting. Jean was moving to Connecticut. I was almost 15; she was a few months younger. It broke my heart to have to say good-bye. She walked over early one evening, and we knew that her grandfather was going to come get her in half an hour. I had put the babies to bed. We sat on the stairway that led to the den. On an impulse that I think I understood more than I really wanted to, I put my arm around her shoulder. I longed to do that—to do more, although I wasn't exactly sure what. It was my first *homoerotic gesture*. I pulled her to me sideways, just a little, sitting next to her on the stairs. I loved Jean; I hated that she was leaving me. I wanted to touch her. I did.

Twenty-five years later, Jean and I would finally talk about that moment and others like it that had shaped our adolescence. Jean told me that she had searched for pictures of the feeling she had when I had held her. The closest thing she had found was a classic picture of Jesus touching someone in a gesture of healing. I cried when she wrote to me about that. (Speaking of repression, Jean told me the fact that she'd made a religious connection to my touch was probably why she found MCC before she found her clitoris!) Jesus, touch, sexuality. Watch out, Nancy, they're going to go nuts!

The hard part for me as an adolescent was that I could not afford to know that my longing to touch Jean was about my sexuality. So I repressed my natural, developing lesbian sexual longings or compartmentalized and mislabeled them. Then I waited for the heterosexual desires, lust, to sort of *happen* to me. It never quite did. Not clearly, and not enough. So I kept waiting and waiting and meanwhile became a great student and a musician. I also got into religion. I kept very, very busy.

I remember going to the movies to see D. H. Lawrence's *The Fox* with the woman who would eventually become my first partner. We were probably juniors in college at the time. I had never seen a woman kiss another woman on the mouth. This film contained one scene in which a woman actually kissed another on the mouth in a *prone position*. I cannot describe my mixed feelings of excitement, anticipation, and terror, and I remember covering my face with my hands and peeking through. Then, in an instant, it was over. No one died. I do, however, remember the noises of disgust from the audience. It really didn't look strange or awful to me. And I didn't want to think about that!

Part of healing and coming out for me was the process of "un-re-pressing," actually uncovering the truth about sexual feelings, touching, arousal, and pleasure. I was learning to find out for myself, not to take anyone else's word for it—not even D. H. Lawrence's. I was beginning, day by day, to throw off the projection, the fears. I'm still learning how to do it.

I had to learn that there is nothing particularly exotic or weird about homosexuality. I had to learn to recover from my own sexual and emotional isolation; to recognize sexual arousal, erotic impulses, and fantasies in myself; to learn how my own body likes to touch and be touched. I had a lot of remedial work to do. I had starved myself sexually, because I thought this would keep me from being punished and despised.

If sexuality is a part of life, a gift to help us be more fully alive, Jesus must have included sexuality in his promise, "I came that they may have life and have it more abundantly" (John 10:10).

After I came out, and came into MCC, I immediately had to deal with sexual projection. On top of being an open lesbian, I came out publicly almost immediately as a lesbian clergy, a pastor in a gay church. In the late fall of 1972, my picture appeared on the front page of the city section of the *Boston Globe*: instant public queer at age 22.

In about 1974, when I was pastoring MCC Worcester, I got a call from someone who wanted to talk to me. We had no church office, except in my kitchen. For reasons of safety, I didn't meet strangers in my home very often, but, when I did, I always made sure that my partner or another member of the church was present. For some reason, it was more convenient to have this man come talk to me in my kitchen, while my partner waited in the living room.

A mousy-looking older white man appeared at my door, looking a little anxious. He sat in my kitchen, hemmed and hawed, then began telling me about himself. He had asked me early on if I was a lesbian, and I had said yes. He then told me about a visit to a massage parlor in western Massachusetts, and, over a long half hour, he told me that a woman there had given him an enema, which he had found sexually stimulating. It turned out that this was a *new* experience for him (and, because I had never heard of such a thing, it was becoming a new experience for me!). The massage parlor had been closed down. He also thought that *this* woman was a lesbian. So, finally, he got around to asking me if, because I was a lesbian, would I be willing to give him an enema?

Well, no one at Boston University School of Theology had prepared me for this type of pastoral counseling inquiry. I continued to manage my facial expression while clearly and firmly telling him that I would not be willing to give him an enema. Also, I informed him that I was afraid that he did not have a very good understanding of what a lesbian was and that I was the pastor of a church—you know, a place where people sat in pews (or, in our case, on folding chairs), sang hymns, listened to a sermon, took communion, and went home. No enemas.

Actually, I was neither sarcastic nor unkind. I felt sorry for him because he did not quite know how to get his needs met. On some level of human connection, I certainly understood. I told him to ask for help at a particular notorious bookstore in town that might have "referrals." (I bet the Lutheran pastor in town would not have been able to handle it that way!)

It did shake me up just a bit, though, to think of the many fantastic and unusual ways in which people viewed me (and other MCC or gay and lesbian clergy). In some ways, I feel like I am a modest, rather conventional person in my sexual needs and expression. In the Seventies, especially, MCC clergy were often the only openly gay people in their city or town. This is *still* true in the more rural areas of the United States and in other countries. We had to know more than we might have wanted to know about lots of different sexualities, including (as I found out) information about enemas, sex toys, and bookstores. We spoke at colleges and health classes about our sexuality. We had to learn to speak publicly and comfortably about male and female anatomy and sex practices and how to handle homophobic, ignorant, hostile questions and comments. Over and over and over, we were taught as MCC clergy such things as how to put our books about sexuality at eye level in our offices so that parishioners would feel comfortable enough to talk with us about their sexuality. We were to model healthy and open attitudes about sexuality in our words and behavior.

Our parishioners *did* talk to us about sexuality a lot. We helped them come out, and we helped them talk about relationships, dating, sexual hang-ups, guilt, and fear. It was a kind of on-the-job training: everything you wanted to know and more—much more.

We had to try to help others heal and be comfortable with their sexuality while we were still discovering ours. It's amazing that people survived our early efforts.

I discovered that people are sometimes curious about the sex lives of clergy, including gay clergy. Sometimes people have assumed that I'm celibate (they think I'm a nun). This has been true for heterosexual Christian clergy as well. Troy used to say that, when he was in the Church of God of Prophecy, heterosexual male members of his church would boast and hand out cigars when they had fathered a child. When a clergyman fathered a child, however, it was sort of a big secret. The child was a gift from God, as if sex had nothing to do with it.

Sometimes I am surprised by how easy it is for some people to talk about their sex lives and how difficult it is for others. For some people it is a lot harder and even more intimate to talk about their spiritual lives than it is to talk about their sex lives.

People also have incredible psychological *transference* issues with clergy—something I never learned about in seminary. And it's even more complex when you are a clergyperson in a sexual minority community. We are only beginning to know how powerful the role of a clergyperson is in our culture. My experience is that many people project onto me their fears and wishes about God. I think people do this to one degree or another with all clergy. I remember how hard it was for my mother to call the assistant pastor of the church we attended by his first name. He was her age and a kind, committed pastor. But clergy had this aura, this mystique. They weren't quite human in a relaxed sort of way, and maybe we didn't want them to be.

Because clergy are authority figures, they sometimes abuse that authority. Clergy also have a lot of difficulty managing the role. We think we're supposed to be perfect, have perfect families, and never have doubts or weaknesses.

People come to my office saying they are afraid of me and don't know why. Usually it's because they were afraid of a clergyperson from early in their life, or, more probably, they are afraid of God. Or they fall in love with me as they are falling in love with God. If they hate God, they sometimes hate me—after all, they can *see* me!

I have had to learn ways to hold up a mirror and help people see what their feelings about me *tell them about themselves*. Mostly, thankfully, the transference really has nothing to do with me! But, if I am needy or vulnerable, I may forget that fact.

I meet many women and men who were molested or abused by clergy or church leaders, some of whom were their parents or relatives. It is extremely hard for them to think that they can ever trust a religious authority figure again.

In many ancient cultures, gays and lesbians were *not* the objects of sexual projection, at least not in a negative sense. Native Americans call gays the "two-spirited people," meaning that they have both male and female *spirits*. Gays and lesbians were often seen as specifically blessed. Rather than cursed as "half a man" or "half a woman," they were "double" people—blessed with the wisdom of seeing life from both male and female perspectives.

So how are we (modern gay men and lesbians and other sexual minorities) to see ourselves? As broken or as gifted? As both? As wounded healers of our culture's sexual repression-obsession polarity?

Gay men and lesbians are in a sense *forced* to work on our sexual healing just to survive in a homophobic culture. The world needs to know what we have been learning while we have been healing. Because what we have learned together and who we've become as we've learned it are the source of tribal gifts we long to offer to the world.

2 • Boldly Exercising Our Tribal Gifts

It is an audacious thing, at this crucial moment, to claim purpose and meaning for gay and lesbian people on the planet. How unbelievable to claim that those who were labeled sick, perverted, criminals, and the *foulest* of sinners could have personal, cultural, spiritual, and, yes, tribal gifts to share!

Part of moving beyond projections is to assert who we are *not* and who we *are.*

We are *not* an aberration. We are not a deformity or a mistake. We are not a genetic deficiency that needs to be tolerated or eradicated. We are not an annoying group of sex fiends seeking to legitimize perverted sex in the streets or the schoolyards.

We *are* a necessary part of creation, biologically, sociologically, and spiritually. We, like others—no more and no less—contribute to the wholeness, the multidimensionality of creation. Neither creation nor the church is complete without us.

Just to prove this point, some of us have had fantasies for years about what it would be like if all gay, lesbian, and gender-nonconforming people were suddenly visible one day, if we all turned purple at once, and could not hide what a large minority we are, or if we all just had a massive walkout one day. Now, when I claim that we have tribal gifts, it is not accurate or necessary to say that *all* queer people have these gifts in equal measure or will necessarily choose to exercise them. But we seem to bear them together.

Gift Number 1: Coming Out

First, we offer the gift of *coming out.* The expression "to come out" is now used generically. It has already been co-opted by the dominant culture. It simply means to tell the truth, to *disclose* the hitherto private, hidden realities of our lives. People come out of the closet about all kinds of things these days, and sexuality is only one of them.

We gay and lesbian people were told we'd better lie to survive. But lying about our sexuality made us sick and afraid. And sometimes it inured us to the act of lying itself. I remember that, in the bar culture of my early coming-out days, many people had aliases or nicknames. You just assumed you probably didn't know people's real names or where they really worked or the *real* story of their lives. One had to suspend judgment, not ask too many questions, and not get caught believing too many lies. For some, lying became positively an art form, almost as if, in *requiring* us to lie, the world didn't deserve the truth from us. Sometimes, in sadly surreal ways, there was more truth in our lying than in the facts that passed for truth. Before the days when sobriety began to heal us, we hardly even held each other accountable for the lying. A lot of it was harmless, anyway, or so we thought. However, we really didn't *like* ourselves when we were liars. So we've stopped lying. We paid dearly for the privilege of telling the truth and gained greatly. The truth is costly sometimes. But it is worth it. I'm not sure if I have ever met anyone who has ultimately regretted coming out, no matter what price he or she paid. Of course, those who died telling the truth about their sexuality or gender identity must be vindicated by our own truth telling.

All queer people can take courage in Jesus' words, "You shall know the truth, and the truth shall make you free" (John 8:32). Now, I know that he meant the truth about himself and who he was and is. But he said *the truth.* As if all truth *is* connected. Like there aren't different kinds of truth. Every truth connects to, and somehow supports, every other truth. To follow Christ is to live in the truth, the whole truth. When the church, or any group or community, tells people that their participation depends on their willingness to lie about who they are, that is degrading and un-Christ-like.

It is so difficult to think about all the people who went to seminary, got ordained, and pastored a church while lying about their sexuality. I'm not only talking about not mentioning it or hiding it from view but also blatantly denying it and lying about it—and persecuting LGBT people to protect themselves.

Others lead double lives while "working for acceptance for gays and lesbians from within." From within what? From within a system of lies, which rewards lying and liars? My bias is that, if you're not ready to come out, don't lie to get into seminary, to get ordained, or to get a job in a church. Wait until you can tell the truth and pay the price.

Lying is soul killing. Jesus did not ask us to lie in order to serve him, or God, or the church. Lying squanders of one of our most treasured tribal gifts: telling the truth, coming out when it is can make a difference. As Lutherans, Episcopalians, Presbyterians, Methodists, Catholics, Mormons, Mennonites, and others emerged with truth-telling over many decades, we have seen a shift. Prohibitions are dropping, and understanding is growing. We have seen the results and need to help churches throughout the world see that truth-telling is life-giving.

Why is it so hard to tell the truth in the church? When Marie Fortune first made a presentation to the National Council of Churches on issues of domestic violence as a problem in churches, I watched the audience shut down, as if to say, "No, no, no, don't force us to hear this." The church does not want to hear the truth about its own complicity in violence—toward children, women, gays and lesbians, or anyone else.

M. Scott Peck, in *People of the Lie*, did a lot to help me understand the connection between psychology and spirituality in the *diagnosis* of human evil.[9] Peck says that the connection between lying and evil is a complex and profound one. When anyone asks or encourages someone to lie, he or she exposes that person to the *tools* of evil. In a sense, the truth is our spiritual equivalent of an immune system. To lie, to encourage lying as a strategy for handling problems, is to compromise our spiritual health. What might the connection be between diseases of the physical immune system and political and psychological oppression, including the rewarding of lying?

Conversely, to tell the truth is to increase our spiritual health. There is a saying in the therapeutic community: "We are only as sick as our secrets." I believe this is why LGBT people need to tell their coming-out stories over and over again. After all the fear, lying, and hiding, telling the truth is positively sacramental. It is a rite of purification. We need to bathe and bask in the truth. I think I am most angry about the way in which homophobia at its core has exposed my people to the spiritual disease of lies and lying. We are those who have suffered the oppression not so much perhaps of compulsory heterosexuality but of compulsive lying. The truth is making us free, and becoming truth tellers is a great gift we bring. Any state, church, institution, or individual who *encourages* LGBT people to lie in order to survive (or to "succeed") contributes to the vulnerability of our people to disease and spiritual or psychological sickness.

Gift Number 2: Same-Sex Eroticism

Harry Hay calls homosexuality *subject-subject sexuality*[10]—that is, as opposed to *subject-object sexuality*. Now, the truth is that gay and lesbian people are just as capable as anyone of sexually objectifying another. And there are heterosexuals who, in spite of patriarchy, manage relationships that are not objectifying. However, it is also true that sex in the Western patriarchal model has *more often than not* been about the eroticization of dominance and dependency. In a culture that reinforces beliefs that men and women are *not* equal politically, most heterosexual sexuality, by definition, lacks the possibility of thoroughgoing mutuality and *informed* consent. That's an astonishing perspective that is at the heart of the feminist critique of culture.

I remember first hearing Freda Smith's poem "Dear Dora/Dangerous Derek Diesel Dyke."[11] She spoke of the special passion of touching and being touched by one whose body is *"as known as your own."* Ours can be a sexuality *not* distorted by the politics of patriarchy to *the degree* that heterosexuality still must be. Even within the comparatively nonhierarchical MCC church experience, there is—and must be —a "church within the church" for lesbians. There has been something absolutely transformative about my relationships with powerful lesbian women who are taking the texts of Christianity, the sacred elements of our tradition, into our own *lesbian hands*. We are daring to uncover the connection of the erotic and the spiritual. The patriarchal, heterosexual model said that friendship was never sexy. But the eroticism of friendship is one of the wonderful tribal gifts we, as gay and lesbian people, bring.[12]

MCC holds regular clergy and leadership conferences to provide continuing education and mutual support. Really, though, these meetings were just an excuse to see our friends—to see the only other people in the world who were trying to make the queer church with our bare hands, no money, and few resources—except, of course, the resources of our courage and creativity. So we came to Camp Letts (YMCA) in the spring of 1982 in rural Maryland.

Partway through our several days together, someone from the YMCA noticed that we were gay. The camp director with whom I had negotiated months before had moved on. The new director claimed to be totally surprised by who we really were. The camp authorities tried to make us leave. We had to interrupt our conference, which included the presence of Dr. Jim Nelson (author of *Embodiment*, and a pro-gay heterosexual seminary professor), to strategize about what would happen if they tried to remove us forcibly. They never did. But the whole experience has been sometimes referred to as "Camp Letts Not."

That was one of the dramas that characterized the week, but there was another. Tensions between male and female leadership in MCC are always present and are more visible at certain times than at others. AIDS was just barely beginning to be understood and experienced at this point.

One of the dynamics that MCC leaders, both clergy and lay, always have to deal with is the heterosexism that creeps into our interactions. Because we are mostly gay and lesbian in MCC, we somehow imagine that we are *exempt* from the dangers of falling into heterosexist roles and patterns. Well, forget it! Whenever men and women in MCC work together, we have to face and identify the inevitable ways in which heterosexual patterns subconsciously emerge. Women assistant pastors in MCC will often find themselves playing the role of wife and mommy to men pastors. Or sometimes, just for variety's sake, women and men will switch roles, but the roles are still present.

One of the continuous strains in MCC has been the way women often fall into the role of taking care of the men. This can be either overt or subtle. In the age of AIDS, the pressures to take care of men have been incredible for women in our church. These pressures have driven some women away. But they existed prior to AIDS as well. Women were support staff, confidantes, for men. Sometimes we covered up for them. We defended them. We endured sexism from them. We educated them. But, by 1982, a lot of the first generation of MCC lesbian clergy were already weary and discouraged. We were part of the first wave of women clergy in significant numbers in the history of the church! Many of us who were brilliant, creative, outstanding preachers and teachers felt like *failures* as leaders. We thought of this as a personal issue and not enough as a political, historical, and systemic problem.

We blamed ourselves. All the models of pastoring were male. All the books on how to pastor successfully were written by men, for men. Somewhere, inside us, we felt we would never be good enough. And, as proud lesbian she-women, we could never admit this to each other! We were tough! We were superwomen! Well, it was a lie. But a miracle happened at Camp Letts. We started talking about it. Like the old consciousness-raising groups of the early women's movement, we began talking about it. Not that we hadn't talked about sexism or inclusive language or all of that for a long time. But now we were talking *to each other*. So the women got together. And it made some of the men nervous. Some of us were thrilled that Dr. Nelson was there. However, we were also furious that, when a straight white man said the very same things women had been saying for years, the men believed him! Suddenly, dealing with sexism was an *in* thing to do. So the women withdrew. The men felt abandoned because, well, we abandoned them! Not forever, but for this time.

It started the first night, when a few of us sat around in the dorm and one of the women just started crying about her anger, about a particular man she was having a conflict with, about things she felt hopeless about. We were in a circle, more or less, and I said, "Why don't we pray for you?" A novel idea—clergywomen actually praying for each other. Then I thought (emboldened now), "Why don't we kind of *lay hands on* you while we pray?" Uh-oh. This sounded a little weird. Isn't that the stuff Pentecostals did?

But we did it. As we laid lesbian hands on her and began praying, something happened. A sound came from this woman's throat—an explosion of rage and pain, like a huge boil being excised. She sobbed in relief. We were stunned; we held her. It was sort of like we'd landed in the middle of someone else's group therapy session. Then, a little timidly, another lesbian clergywoman said, "Me next." She then told of the pain in her relationship with male colleagues, of her desire to pastor her own church, of her self-doubt. She declared her fears of her own radical feminism. So we took turns praying for her. Once again, we witnessed the explosive rage and pain and relief.

I'm not entirely clear about the sequence of things after this point. We skipped dinner, after praying for two or three more women, and then took a break to go to worship services. But we couldn't wait to get back to our newfound experience.

We took over one dorm room, which meant that some women, who felt a little uneasy, decided to move. We tried to negotiate this so that no one would feel pressured to participate or excluded if they did want to participate. I took the lead in suggesting methods of doing the work. Along the way, women would interrupt me, correct my mistakes, challenge me, and take over from me. Laywomen and clergywomen came to the circle for healing. We eventually split into two circles, the demand was so great. At about three in the morning, my legs got so cramped and sore someone massaged them. But I felt like I had boundless energy and insight. I didn't need to drink or eat or sleep. We continued to pray, cry, laugh, hold each other, push, back off, try again, pray, and heal for hours—all night long, in fact. Some attended part of the conference during the next day, while some took naps. But then we got right back to it that night. Women came for healing of their careers or for their churches, but mostly for *themselves*. They began to talk about incest and abuse in ways I had never heard in my life. This prefigured all the revelations about childhood trauma that we would continue to hear about for the next ten years.

It was incredible, to say the least. We stopped worrying about the men. We turned the full force, power, and beauty of our spiritual energy and lives toward each other. We glowed with a delicious sense of having *spent* ourselves on each other. We lavished our time and love and touch and listening energy on each other's bodies and spirits. We *loved each other into speech and wholeness,* to amplify Nelle Morton's powerful phrase, "hearing into speech."[13]

There were moments of unbearable pain and stuckness, and women struggled with their fears of telling the whole truth—fears that, if they told the truth, no one would believe them. They feared that there would be no one to face it with them, that they would be alone and comfortless before the terror of their past. But we weren't alone. Women who had never laid hands on each other in prayer discovered how gifted we were. We experienced, we failed, and we tried again. Some dropped out at different points, needing to rest, needing to grieve quietly, or needing to give themselves safe space. No one interfered with the natural rhythms of our comings and goings. We were learning together: we tried to be compassionate. Lucia Chappelle, who participated in this experience, wrote the following new hymn to a familiar Christmas carol:

> Silent night, raging night,
> Women weep at their plight.
> Circling nurturers comfort give
> Offering new kinds of spiritual gifts.

Christ's new Body is born,
Christ's new Body is born.

Silent night, raging night,
Ne'er before, such a sight.
Christian lesbians hand in hand
Many theories, one mighty band.
Christ's new Body is born,
Christ's new Body is born.[14]

Many women looked at those days and nights as a turning point. Sometimes, when I think about it, I long for the intensity of that time—that time of a door opening. Some of the learning we did that night survives in the pastoral ministry of dozens of lesbians (and those they've mentored) who have continued to practice the healing arts over the last decade, especially in MCC.

I still think, though, that lesbians, and lesbian clergy in MCC (or the mainline churches), are reluctant to give to each other freely and completely. If we did, would we have to face all the pain of the deprivation we have experienced? Would we have to change the way we do everything? The way we feel about everything? There is something about the power of same-sex eroticism and camaraderie that is essential to the survival of our species in our world. Will the world or the church ever be able to receive that gift?

Gift Number 3: The Humorous Messenger

The "camp meeting" at Camp Letts I described in the previous section included raucous, uninhibited laughter. The healing properties of the physical activity of laughing have been well documented. Also well documented is the place of humor in the LGBT culture.

I can think of no other protest or civil rights movement that has been accompanied by so much self-reflective humor. Mark Thompson writes about this as if it were almost an ethnic or genetic gay and lesbian characteristic in his essay *Children of Paradise: A Brief History of Queens*:

The role of the fool, the trickster, the *contrary one* capable of turning a situation inside out, is one of the most enduring of

all archetypes. Often cross-dressed, or adorned with both mas-
culine and feminine symbols, these merry pranksters chase
through history, holding up a looking glass to human folly.[15]

Hold up a looking glass to human folly. Sometimes humor is a response
to the deadly power of tragedy, and its attempts to rob us of whatever joy
or hope we possess. I can never forget the chant that would inevitably
start at AIDS demonstrations when stone-faced police officers would arrive with their *prophylactic* yellow rubber gloves allegedly to keep themselves
from *catching* AIDS while dragging us away to jail:

Your gloves don't match your shoes,
your gloves don't match your shoes!

Nothing about AIDS is funny—or about the ignorance of the state
and those who police it. But these chanters saw something funny in the
fanciful, ignorant projections of their persecutors and made fun of them.
That humorous way of turning the tables, of laughing in the face of
insults, is simultaneously disarming and empowering.

Sacramento, California, is not known for its architectural or aes-
thetic beauty. So, when hundreds of thousands of gay and lesbian protes-
tors took over the capital in October of 1991, a clever chant mocking the
stereotype of gay interior decorators was designed for the occasion:

We're here! We're queer! Let's redecorate!

One of the worst slanders directed toward gays and lesbians is that
there is something inherently sad, lonely, and pitiful about our life. Or
if there is any humor, it must be self-destructive, a la *Boys in the Band*. I've
known thousands of LGBT people. The sad and lonely stuff is about oppression, not about sexuality—and the cure for that is coming out. Not
that we don't have the same human complaints as everyone else, or our
moments or moods, or neurotic friends!

While at the WCC General Assembly in Australia, we were treated to
an evening of local Australian entertainment outdoors in a nearby park.
Around 3,000 people were present. About ten women from the Christian
Lesbian Collective came down from Sydney to support us, as did MCC
folks from all over Australia and even a few people from New Zealand.

About 30 gays and lesbians sat together that evening on the lawn, amidst
the 3,000, thrilled to have found each other in this big crowd on this

beautiful continent. Those of us from the U.S. delegation were especially glad to have local LGBT support for our presence at the WCC assembly,

We lounged on the grass together, sharing food, stories, clowning, showing off, and introducing ourselves. I sat on the edge of our crowd next to a group of Korean Protestants. The man sitting next to me kept staring at me. We introduced ourselves, just as the program was beginning. He kept asking me questions, and I was a little annoyed at the time. So, probably in hopes of shutting down the conversation, I came out to him about MCC. But this only made him want to talk more. He wanted to know how I knew I was a lesbian and how my family felt about it. His questions felt awkward and intrusive. I finally asked him if we could arrange to have a longer conversation when it was easier to talk. He froze up at the suggestion.

And then I saw it, that familiar look of fear on his face, the look of a closeted gay person. I saw the desperate, strained, starved look, utterly humorless. He finally looked at me squarely and said, "Are you happy?"

I was going to answer just for myself, when a familiar sound caught my attention. It was Rev. Steve Pieters (delegate from MCC to the WCC), waving his muscled arms above his head in a kind of dance, just screaming with laughter about something, the way Steve can be hunky and nelly in the same moment. Everyone around him was in on the joke. They were laughing, hugging, gesturing wildly. These people who had been strangers just half an hour ago were having the time of their lives. I simply turned to my new friend and said, "Do they look happy?"

He looked over the scene (how could you miss it?) and said with the barest hint of a smile, "Yes."

"All of them are gay," I said.

His mouth just opened, wordless. "I see," he finally said. A little tear was in the corner of his eye. He then felt the need to turn back to his group for the rest of the evening. Though we passed each other many times during the assembly, he never looked at me, and I never spoke to him again.

Gift Number 4: Our Shamanistic Gifts of Creativity, Originality, Art, Magic, and Theater

One of the features in my "pastor's bag of tricks" is my magic act. It's not a real magic act. It's pure spoof, zany and a little bit mad. I started doing it at clergy conferences late at night when I was bored or when I felt my colleagues needed entertaining (sort of like my own version of USO). Then it just took on a life of its own! I occasionally perform it while visiting MCC churches or at congregational meetings.

I had loved dressing up and entertaining as a child—but not in the usual ways. Halloween was one of my favorite times. I'd usually dress in some kind of male drag, and then I'd dress up both my brothers and anything else that would stay still long enough. I wrote plays for our neighbor kids and loved to fantasize about being a performer. I didn't feel pretty or feminine, but I knew I could make people laugh. Mostly, I liked making myself laugh.

Once in a while, at serious moments in church, I have a nearly un-controllable impulse to break into the magic act. Preaching and leading worship and consecrating the elements are all magical, and sometimes they just cry out for a *lighter touch.*

There is this persistent stereotype of "gays and the theater": gay mu-sical-comedy queens, not to be confused with lesbian softball as perfor-mance art. One of the functions of gay and lesbian people is that we are the *in-between* ones. Judy Grahn says (in *Another Mother Tongue)* that, in times of great social transformation and upheaval, we carry messages across gender lines. We are the *berdache* (Native American word for gay male or cross-dresser) who patch up broken relationships. We are the *go-betweens* when there are disputes. We are the mediators of conflict and culture. In some ways, we are those who *intercede,* who create the path-way for change, for moving into the next era.

I had a wonderful opportunity to offer this gift at the WCC General Assembly. One of the contexts of the assembly in Canberra in 1991 was the Gulf War. The WCC decided to hold a vigil to pray for the end of the war.

The U.S. delegation (the largest, with 600 people) was to lead the closing hour of the vigil at six in the morning. (This was the Sunday morn-ing before the emotional communion with the Lima Liturgy.) In organiz-ing for the vigil and our participation, Joan Campbell, general secretary of the NCC, had asked for a few volunteers. Well, I knew that, at meetings like this, no one really wants to volunteer for such things. So I volunteered. Joan didn't flinch at all, and I was appointed to the committee, which in-cluded some U.S. denominational leaders and WCC delegates.

Our planning committee met briefly outside the worship tent. Rev. Kit Cherry had made some helpful suggestions. No one else seemed to have any ideas. The rest of the committee's idea of the good use of an hour of vigil time was to read more and more boring statements about how we hate the war. So, to work we went! MCC folks (and some closeted gay members in the group) suggested that we open with a Native American drum call to worship. Then, after some brief testimony and prayer, we could invite people forward for anointing with oil.

We decided to use oil because it was a biblical symbol for healing and for *brotherhood and sisterhood*. We chose Psalms 133:1–2:

> And very good and pleasant it is when brothers and sisters live together in unity!
> It is like the precious oil on the head, running down upon the beard, on the beard of Aaron.

This would also allow us to use, with a sense of irony, a symbol of the painful reality that the buying and selling of *oil* was at the heart of this horrible war.

People seemed to like our suggestion, mostly because they were too stressed and tired to come up with anything else. Those participating then told me they didn't exactly know *how* to anoint with oil, so we did a practice session. Actually, I didn't remember anyone ever teaching me how to do it. It was like I was born knowing how to do this. We suggested using the conference theme as an anointing blessing, "Come, Holy Spirit, renew your whole creation," although I explained that the pastors might want to be free just to pray or bless freestyle, if they felt so moved. Most of them looked utterly terrified by that suggestion.

Then we began to search for blessed oil. No one seemed to have any. I had certainly not brought any with me from the United States. No one on the worship team staff at Canberra had any or knew where to find some. Finally, one of the staff "gophers" told me he knew where to get oil! Kit Cherry and I decided to use her empty film cases as makeshift oil vials, and we got MCC people to hold the vials for the blessors during the time of anointing (so that they wouldn't get distracted by the fact that the oil was in film cases!).

I waited forever for this guy to come back with the oil. Finally, he found me: he had the happy look of one who has successfully completed his mission. He handed me a bottle of baby oil. Baby oil! I could just imagine how distracting it would be to be anointing or anointed with the smell of baby oil all around. Can you imagine having this solemn service in the WCC worship tent—and then anointing people who suddenly feel like taking a nap? "They didn't have any olive oil?" I whined.

"Olive oil?" he said blankly. Holy oil is not supposed to smell like babies' bottoms! But, ever resourceful, our gay spirit rose to the occasion! Steve Pieters just happened to have some frankincense with him. Sure—don't you know people who carry frankincense around with them all the time?!

So I mixed the baby oil and frankincense and put the mixture in the film cases. This did change the smell—well, at least a little. Then we blessed the oil in preparation for the service.

I was comforted by the belief that not very many people would show up at six in the morning for this event. WRO-ONG! Probably more than 500 people were there when it started.

The drumming began, the prayers were said, and then I read the Psalm and talked about how we might transform and restore the image of oil for ourselves that day. How we *needed* to anoint each other and the whole world that morning. And we did. Joan Campbell, Bishop Edmund Browning, myself, and six or seven others began anointing the crowd while an African-American seminarian woman sang, "There is a balm in Gilead, to make the wounded whole."

When the bishop of Baghdad (Baghdad, Iraq, that is) came forward that morning to be anointed by Bishop Browning, the room just broke open in solidarity with our pain and our helplessness. Some were too overcome to keep anointing. They collapsed in sobs, on the floor, in their chairs. People wept, prayed, and hugged, as the mournful sounds of that spiritual continued. Gay and lesbian delegates to the WCC came forward for anointing, hugged me, and came out to me on the spot. The tent was filled with the power and presence of the God who wanted us to transform not only the WCC but the world, who makes a way where there is no way, who longs to turn swords into plowshares.

Many people spoke to me about how moving and *right on* that liturgy was. I felt a bit mystified. To me, it felt so familiar, so ordinary. Not the context, of course—that was overwhelming and extraordinary. But the liturgy, the anointing, the *sensing of the moment*—inventing liturgy to move and express the fullness of the moment—was what we experience frequently at Metropolitan Community Churches. It made me realize how much I take MCC and the gifts of LGBT people for granted. And I loved the *subtext* of the baby oil and frankincense and film case mischief, the humor and joy and the making do with what we have. It serves as an example of, as Harry Hay says, "turning hand-me-downs into visions of loveliness."[16]

There is also that strange phenomenon we affectionately call our *gaydar:* the radar that across a crowded room often allows gay and lesbian people to identify each other. It is not foolproof, mind you.

At one very tense NCC meeting (in Cleveland, Ohio, 1992), MCC and members of the gay and lesbian caucuses pooled our resources and set up a hospitality suite to welcome NCC delegates, create some safe space for ourselves, and have all our literature available. Not many NCC folks showed up.

But I began to notice that people were disappearing from our visitors' table and excusing themselves to "person" the suite. Soon the word came back that, although the NCC was not availing itself of our hospitality, the gay and lesbian hotel employees were! There was a party going on up there, and, as the employees ate up all our food, MCC people shared with them the good news that God does love gay and lesbian people. From that moment on, during the course of the NCC meeting, I could often look across the ballroom and see hotel employees serving coffee to bishops and delegates while rolling their eyes at us!

Harry Hay also reports that "the biologist, Julian Huxley, over half a century ago pointed out that no negative trait [and we know, in biology a negative trait is one that does not reproduce itself] ever appears in a given species millennia after millennia unless it in some way serves the survival of that species. We are a species variant with a particular characteristic adaptation in consciousness whose time has come!"[17]

Gift Number 5: Made In The Image of God

On a visit to All God's Children MCC in Minneapolis, I witnessed a new phenomenon: a gay men's softball team. Now, lesbian softball is legendary and an undisputed part of lesbian culture in the United States. But a gay male team? The MCC in Minneapolis had three teams: two were lesbian, and one was composed of young gay men with shaved, punk haircuts, earrings, and muscled bodies (who wanted to be lesbians when they grow up?). They had a very cute team name—The Altared Boys—and great T-shirts that said:

MADE IN THE IMAGE OF GOD—
not necessarily
YOUR IMAGE OF GOD!

I believe that LGBT people contribute to a more complete picture of God. If human beings are made in the image of God, then that includes queer folk. What about us rounds out the image, do you suppose? Ours is the God who invented truth, who is always *coming out* (another synonym for revelation?).

I've always felt that God has a sense of humor. Much of the humor in the Bible has long since been lost in the translation, quite literally. But "he [sic] who sits in the heavens laughs" (Psalms 2:4). Sometimes I think God plays with me, and we have had some private jokes. For a long time, I was afraid to say that out loud. It seemed so grandiose and self-absorbed. I was too sophisticated really to think of God in those affectionate, personal terms.

Sometimes it's just the incredible, illogical synchronicity of things. During one of the worst years of my life (1977), I was driving in the wee hours of the morning from Fort Wayne, Indiana, to Detroit, Michigan, coming home from a preaching engagement. I had recently ended a four-year relationship that had been deteriorating for some time. In addition, there were some nightmarish events and problems that had affected the church. I was exhausted, demoralized, and felt, in the words of Al-Anon literature, "unwanted, unloved, and alone"—and sorry for myself. I turned on the radio and heard a new song: it was Billy Joel's "Just the Way You Are." Later, I would learn that Billy was from my home town of Hicksville, New York. Billy's Long Island accent was poignantly familiar and tugged at me on that lonely road—as well as the words and the saxophone. I changed the station, and the song came on again. That startled me. A new popular tune, I guessed! I listened to the words again, full of sweet assurances. I began to have this eerie feeling of not being alone in the car. I could feel the tightness in my chest relax and the sadness and depression lift for a moment. In a little while, I turned the dial again—and there it was again. This time it scared me. Okay, it's you. You love me. The tears came, and I started laughing, "Okay, okay, God, you love me. You want to talk to me."

But it didn't stop there. It seemed that every time I walked into a room where a radio was playing, it was on. Other people even noticed it. This went on for months and months. Paula and I were walking through Boston Commons the following summer (we had met just three weeks after my drive from Fort Wayne that night), and a guy was playing that song on a xylophone! Even today, that sweet song appears and interrupts me, especially if I'm feeling a little unwanted, a little unloved, or alone. I don't pretend to understand it; I just try to accept it. The words and tune just sort of befriended me, as a precious gift from a God who thinks I'm too sophisticated for my own good a lot of the time.

Now, it's one thing to claim that God might actually tolerate or accept LGBT people; it's quite another to claim that people might be able to see God in and through us sometimes.

Our church, MCC Los Angeles (now Founder's MCC), had a sort of nervous breakdown about this in the fall of 1989. It was a difficult time. I had been on a 30-day fast (to pull the church together and call attention to the fact that we might be in danger of losing our church property partly because banks won't give mortgages to churches, much less gay and lesbian churches), followed by gall bladder surgery. I had been out for seven weeks. The church had been worried about me. We were successful in saving the property, so we were able to move into the building and to raise enough funds to keep us going for a while, until we finally got that new loan years later.

But the congregation was *weary*. A young, brilliant student clergy was writing the liturgy and preaching for my first Sunday back, It was All Saints Day. He and a small committee had designed an extremely innovative gay and lesbian All Saints' liturgy that they knew might be a *little* controversial. Jim thought I had seen it before it "went to press." I had not. Ten minutes before the services began, deacons came roaring into my office telling me I had to *pull* the liturgy. I finally got to see it. In the call to worship it said, "O lesbian God, O gay and gracious God." It was not my style to pull the rug out from under student clergy, even if I thought they were being wrongheaded about something. I knew that some of the more conservative and evangelical gay and lesbian MCC Los Angeles folks would be disturbed by these words, but I didn't think it was a matter of life and death. So I got up at the beginning of the service, tried just to acknowledge the conflict, and to help us relax and get through it.

Well, it just got worse. I had no idea how frightening and devastating it would be for some people to hear this liturgy. Some folks were oblivious, and some loved the liturgy, but many were simply horrified at the phrase "lesbian God."

Part of the problem was that those from evangelical and conservative backgrounds often have difficulty with metaphorical language about God that you cannot document in the Bible. And another part of it was leftover guilt, shame, and doubt about how God feels about us.

I tried to say, "Yes, but you call God the *rock* of your salvation, and you *know* God is not really a rock." But for them there was a difference between familiar metaphors and this new one. They were partly terrified that someone (some visitor to our church, perhaps) would believe that they were not worshipping the God of the Bible, the God of Jesus, but that somehow this phrase meant they were worshipping their own sexuality. This had been an early stereotype of MCC—that we were not really a church, that we were a cover for a gay "social club" or sex club, or that we were just using the veneer of "church" to justify ourselves. All these were (and still are) painful misrepresentations of our church, which we continually battled. Also, we struggled not to be so exclusively LGBT—so we were afraid that heterosexual people would not feel welcomed and included by this liturgy. For some people, the articulation of "gay God" seemed like self-worship, like blasphemy, like a betrayal. It was just too exclusive, too *out there*.

Interestingly enough, however, it was "lesbian God" and not "gay God" that was attacked. At least with the metaphor "gay God," God was still male. That told me a lot.

I tried to communicate, counsel, and teach about metaphorical language about God. For some of the people who had been upset, this helped. For others, it didn't. Some wanted me to punish Jim, the student clergy, which I would not do. Some used this event to dump all their fears and angers about the fast on me. Some wanted me to say that the lesbian God thing was a *terrible* mistake. I did believe that not preparing the congregation for that liturgy was a tactical mistake, and I would have done it differently if I'd had the opportunity. But I could not say what they wanted to hear: that comparing God to a lesbian or a gay man was a terrible *mistake*.

When I tried to help them hear that God is everything *good* that gay and lesbian people are, just as God is everything good that a rock is, or a lily of the valley, or a shepherd, it just didn't get through.

I tried to say that we are not less like God than a rock, or a tree, or a heterosexual person. But, when I tried to communicate this, I often hit a brick wall—a brick wall called internalized homophobia. My efforts to name it were met with scoffing, denial, and incredibly painful statements such as "calling God a lesbian is the worst thing you could ever call him [sic]." This was spoken by a lesbian.

It broke my heart, and it drove Jim away from the church for perhaps the last time (he'd been Lutheran before he came to MCC). It took a long time for us to understand and process that trauma—really to understand how deep the wounds of internalized self-hatred are in our community. Sometimes, when we are highly affirming about being gay or lesbian, or about being made in the image of God, we simply scare ourselves to death. Somehow, when we see our sexuality as *part of our connection to the image of God*, we feel we will be accused of making God in our image. Or we accuse ourselves before anyone else has a chance to!

Our Spiritual Gifts

These, then, are some of our gifts: *truth telling*, most especially in the form of coming out; *same-sex erotic friendship* as a cultural antidote to the eroticization of dominance and dependence; being willing to be the *humorous messenger; creativity and magic;* and *contributing to a fuller image of God.* All of these, in their own way, are spiritual gifts. But are there other, more specifically spiritual gifts that gay men and lesbians might give to the church? What might be some positive elements in LGBT spirituality?

Pro-Life Spirituality

I would like to use Mary Daly's method of the "righteous rip-off" for this concept! It seems to me that those who have taken the label "pro-life" are often pro-life only up until birth. (They don't support a nuclear freeze, an end to capital punishment, gun control, or universal day care, for example.) Also, LGBT people have been viewed negatively because we are viewed as non-reproductive—as if that makes us somehow anti-family, anti-life. The fact that we don't reproduce without some extra effort means that, when we *do* have children, we want them. And we are willing to care for them. Also, many LGBT people raise other people's offspring, as we always have. (How many straight people were raised by "unmarried" aunts or uncles, many of whom were gay or lesbian?)

In addition, queer people are wonderful aunts, uncles, and godparents to millions of children. We assist parents, providing backup parenting, adult supervision, and companionship for their children. Also, gay and lesbian people are not just human-centered—we dote on our pets and are historically an *earth-friendly* tribe. We are overrepresented in the helping and caring professions and in environmental and other life-centered movements. The fact that we do not ordinarily reproduce as a result of our sexual activity means that we are helping in the efforts to control population! Overpopulation is never pro-life: it is pro-poverty. We are indeed a people who are *singing for our lives,* who know that silence equals death and that action equals life. Reclaiming our love for life and our life-giving self-image is a great spiritual gift we can give to the world and to the church.

An Irreverent Piety

We are probably in a good position to hold up the mirror of reflection to the church especially. We are, after all, the "in-between" folks. We've been both very much on the inside of the church (as its organists, choir directors, pastors, board members, deacons, and bishops) and on the outside, trying to learn how to "embrace the exile," in John Fortunato's famous phrase.

Steve was wearing a lavender clergy shirt and waiting in the lobby for a World Council of Churches meeting to begin. An older Australian delegate approached him and said, "In our church, when someone wears that color clergy shirt it means they are a bishop!"

To which Steve replied, "In our church, it means we are gay!" (That's not entirely accurate, but Steve was being playful.)

The woman did *not* skip a beat and rejoined, "I guess that's what it means in our church, too!"

Over the years, people have sometimes commented on my irreverence. Frankly, I hold back a lot—not because I think God will be offended but because I don't want to be more misunderstood than I already am. But I see irreverence mostly as *play.* When you really trust someone, you can kid that person. You know how far to go. I feel like I have that kind of relationship with God.

Church ought to be a place where people are loved, comforted, and uplifted, but also a place where we are shocked, shaken, and turned around. Also, it must be a place where we can laugh. I'm not talking about giggling or chuckling, but deep, roll-in-the-aisles laughing—not every Sunday perhaps, but frequently. In the Middle Ages, it was the custom to begin every Easter Sunday morning sermon with a joke. It was the day above all days when we were to laugh in church, to laugh at the devil who had been utterly defeated and outsmarted.

In most MCC churches, there will be laughter—in some, a great deal of laughter. Maybe this started because many of us were nervous about being in church and being ourselves all at the same time.

A Spirituality That Makes Creative Use of Suffering

I feel very reluctant to assign meaning to human (or other) suffering—like those who say that everything that happens is "God's will." I fully and completely understand the human desire to do that, to explain, justify, and *package* suffering—especially to give suffering a purpose. But I think that most suffering is terribly arbitrary and that part of its painfulness is that much of it is unnecessary, preventable, and pointless.

Nevertheless, suffering may have its *uses*. In a way, I view suffering as spiritual compost. It becomes the soil in which many things may grow: bitterness, rage, despair, loneliness, and hopelessness; or conversely, compassion, tenderness, openness, kindness, forbearance, and patience.

What grows in our compost heaps of accumulated suffering? It is, after all, what grows, not the compost itself, which may have meaning, purpose, even redemptive value. And, in saying that, I do not mean to imply anything in the way of an equation. The juice may not always be worth the squeeze. Not all suffering is good compost. But now and then we get a glimpse of a divine economy that may be large enough to incorporate and heal the suffering of the world.

I met Lew Adams shortly after I became pastor of MCC Los Angeles. He was an "old-timer" in two senses: he was almost 70 years old, and he had been a member of the church for at least 15 years.

Lew came to my office, troubled because he hadn't been baptized and felt he should be. But, he told me, he didn't feel worthy, and he had a hang-up about it. It was a requirement that you be baptized in order to be a member of MCC, but somehow that had been overlooked when Lew had become a member.

Lew's best friends frequently "pestered" Lew about this baptism thing, and, well, he thought he probably should do it. But Lew told me he couldn't because it reminded him of his father. Lew's father had been a crazy, abusive, religious fanatic who starved his children, subjected them to countless beatings, and who had a bizarre sectarian fundamentalist "Christian" theology. Lew had hated his father. He'd had to eat out of garbage cans as a child. He ran away at age 14. When he was old enough, he joined the navy. He ended up becoming a survivor of the March of Bataan in the Philippines. During his captivity, he personally buried hundreds of soldiers who had died of starvation. Lew was convinced that the only reason he survived was because of his early *childhood training through suffering*. He could eat garbage; he could do whatever it took to survive. Lew volunteered for many things at the church and had a small circle of friends. He was compassionate, serious, and could not bear for anyone to be hungry.

A few years after our conversation, he was diagnosed with AIDS. One day, when he was close to death, he told me that the last few years of his life, with AIDS, had been some of the happiest. He told me he felt fortunate to be one of the few older people with AIDS he had encountered; that, unlike so many, he had lived a long life. But what amazed and shocked Lew were all the friends who had rallied to his side during his illness—mostly LGBT friends from MCC Los Angeles who loved him, prayed with him, kept him company, and took care of him. He loved coming to church and felt such a peace and joy there. Finally, just a week or so before his death, he told me he was ready to be baptized. Several friends gathered around, and there was not a dry eye. Lew had a kind of transcendent joy and presence in those last days. There was also the occasional flash of old anger or grief. It took him a whole lifetime to heal from that religious abuse, but he made it. And AIDS became a means of grace for him, as he learned to receive just a portion of the love he had offered to so many all his life. I will never forget his humility and gratitude in the face of horrific suffering. What brilliant flowers grew from this compost of suffering.

The Gift of a New Lens on the Bible

Finally, I also believe that gays and lesbians have another gift to give to the church: *a new lens on the Bible*. We find ourselves and our ancestors in the Bible. We refuse to believe that love would keep us out. With the diligence of the persistent widow demanding justice, we have demanded that God give us justice. We keep coming back to the Bible and history and conclude that we are part of the story of faith.

Many refuse to believe that God could have created us as wonderfully diverse as we are. I remember a street-corner encounter with fundamentalists in West Hollywood. But first, a little background information:

One night, I got a call from Connie Norman. Connie was a mad and brilliant transgender earth mother to all LGBT, AIDS, and justice activists, especially the young ones. Connie was someone who knew how to call out the troops for an action or demonstration. She was always able to get my attention!

Connie was calling every organization she could. I happened to be in my office and decided to drop what I was doing and join the AIDS demonstration at a Federal Building. When I got there, the crowd was growing. I jumped in, and Bob Lucas, Connie, and I handcuffed ourselves to the building. We waited about five hours for the feds to come and arrest us. When they finally came to get us, they took me first. Connie knelt and began praying the Lord's Prayer. I felt like she was doing it partly for me. I'll never forget how it touched me to be supported in that way.

They dragged me for a bit, and the very butch female federal agent said in a commanding voice, "Nancy, just stand up!" I was too dazed and stressed to wonder how the heck she knew my name but not too out of it to disobey! They had run out of paddy wagons and were shoving us, handcuffed, into the backseats of patrol cars. Wayne Karr, AIDS activist and an outrageous person in his own right, was right behind me, not cooperating in the slightest. They had to drag him handcuffed all the way to the car. It was apparently too difficult to shove him right side up into the backseat. So they shoved him down with his face on the floor of the backseat and his feet in the rear window. Actually, most of his face was on my shoe. I kept asking him if he was all right. He laughingly said he preferred my foot to the floor of the patrol car!

So, when I got another call from Connie, I knew I was in for an adventure. This time she told me that a group of fundamentalists were out late on Friday nights handing out antigay literature, pamphlets that said cruel things about people with AIDS and how God feels about them. Connie said, "It's getting pretty heavy out here, and I think the kids"—the mostly younger gay and lesbians and AIDS activists, Queer Nation and Act Up folks—"need to see some collars out here!"

So I took a couple of MCC members and clergy with me on that Friday night at about eleven o'clock to a corner of West Hollywood Park.

There they were. We could hear the din. There were a handful of fundamentalists surrounded by a very loud, screaming crowd of queers. Apparently, this had gone on for weeks and had started out with rational discussions in normal tones. But it had really escalated by now. As we approached, Connie saw me, grabbed me, and pushed me in front of the fundamentalists, saying, "Here's one of our ministers; talk to her!"

Frankly, it was hard to hear ourselves think. But we began to try to talk to them while also acting as a buffer between them and the screaming crowd.

I had to think fast about why we were there and how we were going to handle this. Our crowd (the queers) were so enraged and volatile that I knew someone was going to get hurt. And when that happened someone would be arrested, and it would be someone from our side. I knew we needed to defuse this situation and get these folks to leave the neighborhood. It was clear to me that the fundamentalist leader had some deep personal agendas that he was working out and had gotten some young idealistic fundamentalists to follow him out there to "save" these homosexuals. They felt like they were being "persecuted for Jesus' sake" by this angry crowd. I really believe they had no idea how hostile their activities were. By coming into the small neighborhood of West Hollywood—one of the *only* LGBT-identified cities in the world, just a few square blocks of relative safety and openness—they were *violating* our sense of peace and safety. We lost our safety from bigotry and insult, as well as from physical harm. The fundamentalists had invaded West Hollywood with judgment, condemnation, and pity, all "in Jesus' name"—thinking that was love!

I also surmised that a lot of the queer folks on the street were working out their issues on these fundamentalists. How many of these men and women were preachers' kids or were themselves from conservative religious backgrounds or victims of religious abuse? Even for dedicated activists, it took a lot of commitment to be here every Friday night.

We tried to defuse things by standing between the two groups and engaging the fundamentalists. It unnerved them suddenly to have people talking to them who were not shouting, and who actually knew something about the Bible, and who had in common with them that we would say the words *God, Jesus,* and *Bible* without expletives attached.

I took on the leader and attempted to give him our view of the stories of Jesus in the Bible. Jesus *never* exercised his ministry in a way that made the materially or spiritually poor, the outcasts, feel *worse*. In fact, Jesus criticized the Pharisees, who heaped their judgmentalism and narrow interpretation of God's law on the poor outcasts. The leader asked me if I thought the gay folks were behaving in a very *Christian* manner. I said, "No," but they weren't claiming to! And what kind of treatment had they received from so-called Christians?

By now, Richard Davis, Sandy Williams, Rev. Joseph Gilbert, and others of us had our hands full. The leader seemed more than a little shaken. He made noises like they might want to leave, and we got someone to call them a cab immediately. Then we escorted them to the main street. At one point, the leader attempted to put his hand on the shoulder of an angry young man, who screamed back at him. I took a big chance and with both hands grabbed the young man's shoulders and said, "Cool off; they're leaving." He turned to me with a look of joy and said, "How did you convince them that we are right?"

Well, of course, I hadn't done any such thing. I had only convinced them that this was not a safe or welcome place for their ministry. Freedom of speech does have its limits and responsibilities. Later, the leader of the fundamentalist group tried to sue the police department and the city, saying that they had been battered in some way. I had to testify to the sheriff's department about my own observations to the contrary.

But the young man's response haunted me the most. It amazed and saddened me how much he wanted the fundamentalists to change their minds! He seemed desperate for them to give him some kind of love, approval, or validation that he hadn't gotten or wasn't getting elsewhere. There is this hunger for acceptance and legitimacy that underlies some—but not all—of the rage I saw that night and have seen many other times. That this young man wanted validation from fundamentalists shocked me.

Part of moving toward a positive queer interpretation of the Bible means being willing to move ahead without the approval of fundamentalists and without converting them! No one is going to make this effort, this reclaiming of the Bible, easy for us. Nor can we make it comfortable for them—for fundamentalists, Lutheran bishops, Presbyterian pastors, or even the pope.

We move ahead, and many let go of religion and the Bible because it's just too painful. But, even so, they will call us in the middle of the night to challenge judgmental Christians because somehow, even though we are Christian ministers, they trust us. We are *their* religious queers!

3 • Seismic Theology

Quaking In The House of God

At 4:31 A.M. on January 17, 1994, all of us in Los Angeles and the surrounding region were jolted out of our sleep by a particularly violent earthquake. Years of earthquake preparedness and all the efforts to shore up buildings and infrastructures actually worked remarkably well. A similar size and type of earthquake in India in recent times killed 10,000 people. "Only" about 60 perished in what has been called the Northridge quake. Angelinos were unusually calm in the moment, and there was little criminal activity or exploitation of the event at first. (I can't say that about insurance companies or government agencies later on!)

About a month later, I had a friend introduce me to California Institute of Technology's earthquake spokesperson, Dr. Kate Hutton. Kate is the calm scientist who often appears on behalf of Cal Tech on local and national television just after a quake. She is also an open lesbian.

I have always found that endearing and reassuring in a strange kind of way: Kate's face, sometimes her hair still in the early stages of waking up, and her calm voice speaking with "lesbian authority" about the nature and size of a particular seismic event. Thank God someone understands this, and she's a lesbian! Also, she would often be attired in some kind of feminist or lesbian T-shirt. I would find myself squinting and trying to *read* it on the screen! Which year women's festival T-shirt is she wearing today?

So I got to meet Kate. I wanted to meet her because I was personally more traumatized by this earthquake than by previous ones, and I was trying to learn more about earthquakes, hoping that this would make them less frightening.

My approach to overcoming my earthquake fears is based on my goddaughter Rechal's methodology of facing up to major phobias. Rechal was frightened at an early age by the idea of sharks (she had apparently never actually seen one). At age five or six, she would approach the lifeguard at the beach in Santa Monica and ask, "When was the last shark sighting here?" Then she began to read about sharks. She became so fascinated with sharks that she could tell anyone who cared to listen about the various typologies of sharks, shark habitats, just how dangerous they really are or aren't. She came to believe that sharks, in fact, were actually *terribly* maligned creatures and decided that she might want to become a marine biologist someday.

Not that I am about to become a seismologist. But I thought that maybe just viewing all the equipment and charts and graphs at Cal Tech and all the people at work assembling data on the computers would at least give me the illusion that someone (like Kate?) was "in control" of all this. Actually, in the course of our conversation, Kate told me that, on a particularly slow news day after the earthquake, several news stations got together and asked her, "Did God cause this earthquake?" She told them modestly enough that that wasn't her field of expertise. So much for illusions of control.

The other reason I came to see Kate was to ask her a favor. Our church building had suffered severe damage in the earthquake. We were located just one and a half blocks from the section of the Santa Monica freeway that collapsed. The 70-year-old dome of our historic building (once a famous restaurant located near MGM studios) fell into the street. Fortunately, at 4:31 in the morning no one was around. No one was hurt or killed. But the building had to be torn down. Because we had not finished all the renovation, and because it was an old brick structure, and, even though we had invested more than $100,000 in retrofitting, we were not eligible for earthquake insurance. It was a devastating loss—the second for our 25-year-old church, which lost another building to arson in 1973.

So, I had a brainstorm. If other lesbians and gays were as reassured as I was by "Kate from Cal Tech," we could sponsor an event that would be a fund-raiser. She agreed to give an earthquake lecture sponsored by MCC Los Angeles for the community. Perhaps others, like me, would want to use Rechal's counterphobic approach to their earthquake jitters. Let's get lots more information from our favorite lesbian science teacher!

Plus, I was doing research on the emerging "earthquake theology." It was amazing, in the days and weeks and even months following the earthquake, the kind of earthquake theologies that appeared everywhere. Tony Alamo, a notorious off-the-wall fundamentalist of sorts (a Hollywood fix-hire, really), printed a special pamphlet for the occasion, littering our windshields and the streets of Hollywood with his self-serving diatribe entitled simply "Earthquake." In it, he claimed that God got him out of Los Angeles and saved his life that day. Pat Robertson, Jerry Falwell, and others took great glee in letting us know that the earthquake was God's judgment on Los Angeles, particularly for the sins of abortion and homosexuality. Jerry, in fact, had a video titled *Hollywood, Washington, and Hell* illuminating the connections among the three. In fundamentalist theology, Hollywood was just getting what it deserved. (So what terrible evil and sin were going on in Northridge? Or did God just miscalculate by a few miles? Did God mean to *hit Hollywood* but hit Northridge instead?)

Does God Cause Earthquakes?
Spiritual Narcissism and the Alternatives

So, did God cause this particular earthquake, and why? Is Los Angeles a modern Sodom and Gomorrah, as Falwell was fond of implying? Did our earthquake-preparedness efforts thwart God's plan to kill more of us, or was this just a warning to change our evil ways?

If for the fundamentalists this was the act of an angry, judging Father God, there were some equally firm speculations from a different theological viewpoint. A liberal feminist colleague and friend of mine referred to the earthquake as an expression of "Mother Earth's anger." I have heard this many times in many forms: that earthquakes, floods, and so on are a response to human pollution of the earth, air, and water. Perhaps this is happening because the earth is *sick* of us humans and is trying to warn us or stop us from destroying the environment. Sometimes, this is explained scientifically (if we destroy the ozone layer, for example, then we are "reaping what we sow" in terms of cancer and other life-threatening consequences). Sometimes it is explained mystically (as in my friend's observation).

Was the earthquake about anger and judgment? This seems to be a common theme, even if there are different ideas about just *who* was angry and about *what* precisely. This is a sort of cosmic ACA (Adult Child of an Alcoholic) experience for human beings: we can never be quite sure which parent is going to be in what mood and just when Father God or Mother Earth will decide to fly into a rage and hurt us! And will they hit the right one or just the kid who happens to be within reach? (As Northridge was apparently in the way when God was after Hollywood?)

Are the gods crazy or angry, and how can we appease them? The more optimistic among us began reframing the earthquake as a *good thing*, and we had some great justifications—the minimal loss of life, for instance. Most of us (not *all*, however) were grateful for the timing, when so few people were on the freeways or in office buildings. Also, the search began for the *good results* that often come out of tragedies: people bonding and working together, new focuses on new issues. But this "it was a *good* thing" argument angered a lot of people who felt like they were not allowed to feel grief or anger if thousands were not killed in the earthquake. It reminded me of all the platitudes and clichés some people seem to need to say in the face of tragedies: "Only the good die young"; "God must have needed him or her more than we do"; "Just have another baby right away"; "Something good must be just around the corner"; "Every cloud has a silver lining." Many people need to control what other people feel—the fear seems to be that, if we *all* were to express our grief and loss as they are felt, the avalanche would overwhelm and destroy us. So we counsel each other to *stuff* it, to suppress it, to bury it—but, for God's sake, don't tell us about it!

Eighty churches were destroyed or damaged in Los Angeles during the Northridge quake. But I do not believe that any Baptists or Lutherans or Catholics worried that the earthquake destroying their building meant that God hates Baptists, Lutherans, or Catholics. Yet there *were* members and frequent attendees of MCC Los Angeles who jumped to the conclusion (which obviously already had a foothold in their consciousness) that God allowed the earthquake to destroy our building because *God hates homosexuals.* It was their own mini-Sodom experience, and it is not possible even to explain all the ways that this was played out in our church. Some people simply never came back to the church; others suffered silently, feeling guilty for some time until enough of us had articulated our fears and doubts to give them permission to express theirs as well.

I have heard psychologists talk about the fact that, for many children who are abused, it is more comforting for them to believe that they *caused* or *deserved* the abuse they received than to have to face the possibility that

Daddy or Mommy just beat them because they were *there* or were in the way of their rage. Children prefer to hold on to the illusion of logic or reasonableness rather than to know that they live with powerful adults who do terrible things for complex reasons that have nothing to do with them. This is rooted in the kind of childhood narcissistic view of the world in which "I" am the cause of most things. Children often rely on a kind of magical thinking—the idea that, if they simply wish or fantasize something, it *can* and *will* happen. This is why children often blame themselves if a family member dies or if parents get divorced. "It must have been my fault," they argue. "I did something to cause this." Which means, of course, by implication: "I could have done *something* to prevent this." Which means "the universe is still *somewhat* in my control. If I change now, I can prevent this or other tragedies—if I am just clever enough, or good enough, or smart enough. And if I can't prevent these tragedies, it must be my fault."

Many adults have a very narcissistic spirituality. I believe that this is true partly because many adults' only context for theological reflection is through memories of their early childhood church or religious experience; consequently, when these adults think about God or spirituality, they have only a childhood vocabulary, with childhood images, stories, and experiences to rely on.

Those early childhood images are very powerful. They stay with us even when they are challenged by adult experiences. Many adults who understand (as much as any layperson can, in a scientific sense) the structure of the solar system or the galaxies *still* spiritually dwell in a three-story spiritual universe in which heaven is "up" and hell is "down." These world views (childhood and adult) exist side by side in our consciousness. What many adults do is to tell themselves they just don't believe in that "God stuff" anymore, that they are atheists or agnostics. The problem is, the spiritual narcissism persists beyond our desire to wish it away. When there is a crisis, sometimes older children or adults will unconsciously reach for the spiritual "toys" (or tools) that they think they have long since put on the shelf or in a closet.

An awful lot of adults simply stop growing in their spirituality. When push comes to shove, or the earth shakes, or tragedies come, all that is available to them is a very narcissistic view of God and the universe—the old worn-out toys.

We live in a world that is desperate for adult spirituality and reflection, which can move beyond and heal the latent spiritual narcissism that is *inadequate* for adult living. This explains the popularity of Harold Kushner's book, *When Bad Things Happen to Good People*, and M. Scott Peck's book, *The Road Less Traveled*.[18] Kushner's title is interesting because it uses simple words and is a phrase that plays on a childlike question that all adults have and don't like to admit having: "Why do bad things happen to good people?" Kushner also deals very directly with the second reason I believe we are stuck in a narcissistic spirituality: religious leaders and institutions have failed miserably to foster *adult* faith.

Authoritarian religions are the most obvious about not fostering adult faith. They foster authority-dependent faith based on magical thinking. Fundamentalists and other authoritarian religion systems have a *stake* in adults staying stuck in spiritual narcissism: such persons need a religiously rigid system to hold back adult needs and questions. It is about power and control; it is politically motivated by the desire to keep religious authority figures (pastors, popes, and TV preachers) in power.

On the other side of the spectrum, the more liberal churches and institutions have failed to capture the hearts and imaginations of emerging generations of adults in our quantum age. They do not strive to help adults wrestle in depth with issues of adult faith. This may be out of fear (that there are no answers, that evangelicals are right?) or laziness. It seems to me that most progressive churches seem kind of lost, paralyzed, or floundering, or trying to find something to hang on to, something to live for, to die for. They are struggling to find some anchor of meaning in an age of holocausts, space travel, genetic engineering, sexual revolutions, and terrorism. The "best and the brightest" minds and voices are *not* seeking the church for their vocational venue—at least not as a first career! The church seems like a joke to many, or like a senile parent we don't want to embarrass but we don't quite know how to be honest with him or her, and we don't quite know how to tell them to shut up at the dinner table. The best we can hope for is to restrain them so that they do no harm to themselves or others. But even that is not always successful. So it's not the kind of institution or profession you want to give your life to.

I think many adults feel spiritually orphaned or abandoned by churches all along the spectrum, as adults do by aging parents who are not dead but who are no longer capable or available (if they ever *were*).

I see this all the time in LGBT adults who are trying to find something that *works* spiritually, in the context of a community that turns them on without insulting their intelligence or treating them like children. Both Kushner and Peck's writings are popular not because of the answers they give but because they know *what the real questions are.*

Not everyone, of course, wants a grown-up faith. Many people are so wounded in their spirituality and psyches that they are begging for someone to take care of them, to give them simple answers, tell them what to do, fix it all, touch them, and heal them. It is not easy to form a community with people who want a grown-up faith (but who also have occasional lapses into narcissistic, spiritual longings!) and those who are not strong enough or secure enough to tolerate a more challenging, less dependent faith. I remember one woman at MCC Los Angeles in the middle of a heated theological debate finally saying, "All I want to know about is the Jesus I learned about in Sunday school when I was five!" I understood her pain and her need. But to permit *only that Jesus* is to deprive the church of an adult faith. The truth is, all communities contain a combination of such folks, and all of us move along a continuum of spiritual maturity at different times in our lives. All of us have moments when we are more willing to risk our theologies, when we are open to new information. We all deserve to be met right where we are and to be loved and to be able to hear the Gospel and *grow* in faith at our own pace.

Sometimes it *is* the "little children" (adult or actual) who lead us. Several years ago, as our church began to grow, I was challenged about how my pastoral style would have to change if we were to "break the two hundred barrier," in the language of church growth (in other words, if we were to grow in attendance past 200 to 300). What I was told and believe is true is that I would need to spend more of my time training and mentoring *other* leaders in the church who could share or actually do the pastoring, so that we could nurture and love *more* people.

This meant that I would have to spend 80 percent of my one-to-one time with leaders or potential leaders and only 20 percent of my time with rank-and-file members or with some of the more dependent and needy members of the church who seemed to take an inordinate amount of my counseling time. On the surface, especially to a woman pastor who is supposed to be accepting, warm, loving, and nurturing to the *whole world,* setting these boundaries seemed very *cold.* But I also knew that, if the church were going to move beyond my limits and skills, beyond what I could handle by myself, I had to shift; we had to shift. I had to keep in mind what one teacher had told us: It is possible to give someone a great deal of love, support, and *focused* attention in just five minutes, especially by offering to pray for them.

Then along came my teacher in this matter—a very dependent voice on the telephone. It was a woman who had diagnosed herself as a multiple personality, a self-proclaimed victim of ritual abuse, who wanted me to become her counselor. I did not have the time or skills to do this. So I suggested something. I offered to pray for her once a week for up to five minutes when I was in town. I did this for a year.

Debbie often talked to me in one of her alleged "alter" voices, in a childlike way. She often pleaded for more time and begged me to become her therapist or counselor. Over and over again, I would tell her I was not able to offer her that, but this is what I could offer her: five minutes of conversation and prayer, once per week. Sometimes, she would call the office several times on that day, and the office had to tell her I was not available. Eventually, she was able to stop calling the office as much and only called a lot if I were late or had to reschedule our time. I was always calm and firm. I never went over five minutes. I always reassured her that God loved her and that I was not angry with her. These were my limits; I hoped that she found what I could offer helpful. She always had simple requests for prayer.

It was a long time before I realized that Debbie was *teaching* me about how to shift my style of pastoring; she gave me weekly practice in setting new limits while still offering what I could realistically offer and that in which I was very skilled. During this time, Debbie had one therapist and lost another therapist. She wanted me to fix that, to be her counselor or find her a new one. I calmly declined to help but prayed about it with her. She had financial problems. We discussed options; she had other resources, and we prayed about it. She often wanted me to comment on her diagnosis. That was also inappropriate, and I told her so. I stuck to the program through the constant testing and never changed the boundary. Praying always helped, and sometimes, truthfully, the prayer time was as important to me as to her, though it took me time to see that. That five minutes of prayer often *refocused* me in the middle of a hectic day. It also comforted me when I felt helpless about what I was or was not doing *for* Debbie.

About a month after the earthquake (and several other big losses in my life), I was sitting in my office when Debbie called. I didn't really feel up to it that day. The initial shock of the losses and the earthquake were wearing off. I was feeling inadequate that day and not really sure I was moving ahead in my own pastoring skills. Was I really going to be able to pastor this church? There were still people in the church who felt like I gave too much attention to certain *kinds* of people—people like Debbie. Depending on which group you talked to, you might get a different critique: to some, five minutes was not enough, and it was too much for others. All my people-pleasing issues were in full swing that day. I felt vulnerable, and it was one of those days, and Debbie was on line two.

We talked, and she told me she thought she had a therapist lined up for one month from now, but couldn't I pleeeeease be her therapist? I calmly said no again; we made our next appointment, and I was ready to hang up. Suddenly an adult voice spoke to me on the line, Debbie's adult voice—one of the few times I ever heard it. "Reverend Wilson," she said, "I just want to thank you for all the time you've taken to talk and pray with me. I really appreciate it; you will never know how much."

I took that in and thanked her for being willing to accept what I had to offer. I was humbled, and I felt centered again.

The Measure of Mature Spirituality for a New Millennium

Mature spirituality is tested by several things, primarily how we deal with the tragic, how we deal with the poor, and how we deal with joy and sexuality.

Liberation theology speaks of "God's option for the poor," meaning the economically poor. "God's option for the poor" means that God loves all people, rich, poor, and in-between, but that God asks those who *have* to be in a constant process of conversion and solidarity with those who *have not*. In a world where desperate poverty causes unbelievable suffering, God calls us to change the world, so that their suffering is relieved.

It is dangerous to spiritualize the poor, as if there is not a special way in which we are called to show solidarity with those who are economically oppressed. Sometimes Christians have addressed spiritual or emotional "poverty," metaphorical uses of the word poverty, without ever addressing the causes or cures for economic poverty. This has become a rationale for not caring about the poor. It is important not to *substitute* the term poor (meaning spiritually or emotionally poor) for *economically* poor. On the other hand, I do *not* think it is wrong to *expand* our understanding of the poor to include all who are oppressed—economically, politically, emotionally, and spiritually—while making sure that we understand the *serious differences* between literal and metaphorical poverty. Seeing the connection does not *have* to dilute the truth of God's option for the economically poor, if we are vigilant.

All gay and lesbian people experience oppression. Economic, race, or gender privilege may insulate some of us for a time or to a degree from that oppression, but not always and not forever. So, in the gay and lesbian community we are also poor, although some are poorer than others, and there are certainly the economically poor among us. Indifference on the part of some to the poverty of others is real in the gay and lesbian community.

But how a religion, spiritual path, or church responds to the poor is one measure of its authenticity, its maturity. Its refusal to ghettoize the poor, and keep them out of sight—its refusal to distance itself from the needs, cries, and gifts of the poor—is a measure of how rich a spirituality this really is.

And this is not about romanticizing "the poor." Jesus said he came not for the well but for those who knew they needed a physician. He was not *excluding* the well but asking them to be willing to see what in themselves *still* needed healing, and how they could also join him in seeking those who already knew their need of a physician (of God).

When the church at large refuses to see gays and lesbians as the poor or to reach out, touch, include, and respond to us, it exhibits immaturity in its spirituality. When MCC or other gay and lesbian churches refuse to touch and see the poor among us (those with AIDS and HIV, those in prison, those who are economically poor), we betray the very vision that birthed us.

Also, the way in which our faith is able to embrace the tragic without explaining it away, minimizing it, or allowing it to be the *ultimate* truth is another measure of mature spirituality.

In being willing to deal with and learn from the poor and the tragic, we are engaging in a process of healing the spiritual narcissism that dominates so much of religious life in our culture in this century.

When the earthquake of January 17, 1994, hit Los Angeles, I was in bed sound asleep next to my wife, Paula. When it began, I was terrified, sure that we were going to die and that the house was falling down on top of us. I grabbed Paula and would not let her go. She tried to get us both up and to some safer place, but I wouldn't cooperate. I was terrorized. And then I began thinking that probably other people were dying, and I prayed all kinds of selfish prayers that *everyone* would be all right. Although I said everyone, I think I really meant people I knew. My father had died the month before, along with nine other people I knew (mostly of AIDS). The thought of thousands of deaths, of friends or family or church members dying, seemed beyond my capacity to handle. So, though I was praying for them and considering the possibility that some had been injured or died, I was also being totally selfish. I say this without shame, simply as an experience of myself under stress.

The moments after the quake were deadly silent—except for car alarms going off everywhere. There were no lights or phone, only a radio. The aftershocks came quickly and were terrifying.

I said, "Oh, God," about a hundred times. I kept telling Paula I loved her, afraid I would never have the chance to say so again or she would never have the chance to hear me again. It was apocalyptic, like the end of the world. It felt weird to have survived it at first, like we were in some old rerun of *The Twilight Zone*.

Gradually, information began to arrive in bits and pieces, and the light of dawn came filtering through. Phones worked intermittently. I learned that the church dome was in the street, and I headed off with Paula and Norm (who had almost single-handedly renovated the church) to the site. Driving through Los Angeles streets with no streetlights or signals was eerie, surreal.

As a person who has frequently been asked "why" questions by parishioners and others, I stifled that question in myself. Over and over, I had been there with adults who were facing life's struggles with the question "Why?" and who looked to me. I had tried not to lie to them, to pretend to have answers I didn't have.

A few weeks later, while halfway around the globe in South Africa, I happened to be reading a book about maps called *Mapping the New Millennium* by Stephen Hall.[19] Right in the middle of his book, he deals with earthquakes. At first, I just wanted to throw the book at the nearest wall. But I let myself read on. I had some vague notions about earthquakes—that they were a necessary evil somehow, a very natural phenomenon.

I had never thought or theorized much about earthquakes until I moved to California. In the mid-Eighties, my friend Rev. Dusty Pruitt told me about one of my favorite "pop" theology authors, Agnes Sanford. In her later life, Sanford felt *called* to set aside her human-oriented healing ministry (people began to *irritate* her more and more!) and felt a call to pray for the San Andreas fault. She said that she felt she could do this with the clear understanding that earthquakes were natural and necessary but that she could pray for minimal loss of life and property damage as they occurred. Dusty and I observed ominously that earthquake activity began increasing after Sanford died! Dusty frequently wondered just who it was that was to take Sanford's place (her *mantle)* and why they weren't doing their job!

In Hall's chapter on mapping the earth's core and mantle, he comes very close to explaining the physiological "why" of earthquakes. The explanation involves the observation that the earth, contrary to what we may assume, is asymmetrical, even though it is more or less round. It is not perfectly round but *flawed.* These subtle imperfections, it now appears, are linked to the processes that make our planet, "almost alone in the only solar system we know, alive and dynamic and capable of reinventing itself.... If the internal properties of the earth were spherically symmetric, our planet would be tectonically dead. Asymmetry breathes life into the heart of the planet."[20]

Hall says that part of the job of the map reader is to drop old poses and look at familiar materials in unfamiliar ways. (Could this not also describe the job of a creative—or queer—theologian?) Hall observes that the mantle of the earth, though solid, behaves geologically like a fluid; this "mantle operates as a large, single, indivisible convective cell," and this "convection causes the sea floor to spread, creates ocean basins, builds mountains, moves continents, ignites volcanoes, and triggers earthquakes: it is the pulse of a living planet."[21]

Also it appears that the *"enigmatic border* between the mantle and the molten core"[22] of the earth is the arena where the dynamics critical to the life of the earth take place. This is a *powerful* image of the nature of change and the origins of life and creativity.

I believe that both sexuality and spirituality are connected to that "enigmatic border" of our life and creativity. Sexuality is still a great mystery in many ways. Where else in human experience do the issues of genetics, biology, politics, psychology, ethics, poetry, and even metaphysics intersect? What does it mean to be a woman or a man, to be straight or gay or bisexual or gender nonconforming? The very first things that anyone wants to know about you or me when we are born is our gender and if we are *healthy*. Our gender and our health status shape others' and the world's and our own perception of ourselves from *before we are born*.

Whenever anyone challenges our deeply held assumptions about gender or sexuality, they drag us into that enigmatic border, and this terrifies us. People who do so are often ostracized, punished, or banished.

The same, I believe, is true with spirituality. Spirituality is the "enigmatic border" between the worlds—between heaven and earth. It is that inner space that we occupy simultaneously with our physical existence, the inner world of the "heart," "mind," or "spirit" that has fascinated human beings but has always to some degree eluded us. And we also refer to the world of the spirit as our "spiritual life." The word *life* is used both in the physical sense—as biological life —but also in this other sense, the sense of our spiritual life.

What I began to grasp is that events like volcanoes and earthquakes are evidence of *tectonic* life. Also, it is the fact that our earth is a fluid, molten, unfinished core at the center, surrounded by a mantle that behaves like a living, indivisible convective cell and that creates the *biochemical preconditions for life to exist on our planet*. A "tectonically dead" planet cannot produce the conditions that make life sustainable. Neither is life sustainable without sexuality and spirituality.

Earthquakes are a sign that our planet is alive and can sustain life. The problem lies in the *interpretation*. As the earth shakes with new life, some of us are in the way. Buildings, freeways, human creations, infrastructures, plants, animals, and even humans get in the way of these awesome events, and sometimes they are damaged or die.

I meditated a great deal about this new (for me) information about earthquakes. I have not stopped trembling at the memory of the power of those 40 seconds of terror on January 17, 1994. It is easy for me to understand how many people experienced it as some expression of divine or cosmic anger—God's or Mother Earth's. It was so powerful that it was hard not to personify it. But the geophysiology contradicts this. The powerful roar that I can still occasionally recall was not the roar of anger but the roar of tectonic birthing, *the roar of planetary life itself*. That *does* cause me to tremble!

Earthquakes are actually waves. These waves can travel even through the center of the earth and be felt. I can tell you that earthquakes can move through our core being as well. All our issues about life, death, mortality, and priorities—as well as all our "why" questions, all our fears and our needs—come sharply to the surface in the aftermath of an earthquake. For many people, the sense of physical betrayal (the earth is *supposed* to be solid, not fluid) triggers enormous feelings and memories. We ordinarily walk around with the illusion that the earth is steady, and it is not supposed to move, crumble, or shift sideways beneath us. But that is an illusion. The earth is a flawed sphere hurling through space at fantastic speeds around a minor star. This sphere is not solid but molten at its core, allowing it to be constantly reshaped. This illusion of the static, solid ground is very like the illusion that we are *not* going to die or that we have a right to expect to live 70-plus years or so. These are narcissistic illusions. They don't die easily—sometimes they only die with us.

This is the Big Picture for me. A very important way out of narcissistic theology is to keep seeking the bigger picture in order to understand more and more of what is really going on. At the end of the most violent century in human history, our planet managed to be tectonically alive and demonstrated that fact with particular fervor, it seems. Is this the creation and the Creator's response to what humans are doing (or not doing) on the planet, *simply to assert life?* This may be stretching things too far. Perhaps the assertion of life simply keeps happening, whatever we do or do *not* do.

I recall, however, that at the end of the Sodom and Gomorrah story in Genesis 19 there is the *rain of fire and brimstone.* Was that really a tectonic event? Was it a volcanic eruption (which is akin to earthquakes in its geological purpose)? Is God's response to the violence of sodomy *(not homosexuality)* to burst forth in life? We may attempt to *read into this* as human beings a kind of "micro justice" (justice pointed at individuals or small groups) that God is meting out in these events, but that thinking, that theology, is flawed. At best, I believe there is macro justice, but the micro issues are apparently left for us to sort out.

Job of the Hebrew Scriptures discovered that. His lifelong, comfortable, unchallenged narcissistic spirituality that assumed that God rewards the good and punishes the wicked with timely micro justice *bit the dust* when his world fell apart for no damned good reason that he could see. That experience was the beginning of spiritual maturity for Job—as it was for Rob Roberts,[23] of blessed memory, as it is for all of us who struggle, suffer, and grow.

Earthquakes and Faith Crises across Cultures

For many people in Los Angeles and at our church, the earthquake became a fundamental faith crisis. If we cannot count on God to keep the earth from shaking or to keep our church building standing upright or our homes or lives from being destroyed, what can we count on God for, anyway? I remember reading Paul Tillich's theology in seminary. He wrote about a God who is the "ground of our being." What happens to our faith in the ground of our being when the *ground* is shaking?! Tillich obviously had a seismically insensitive theology!

This faith crisis was acted out in many ways in our church. People who believed they had long ago left behind the *judging* God suddenly found themselves wondering if God was exercising a fundamentalist-style micro justice in toppling the building of an LGBT-owned church building. There was almost a kind of morbid glee when our members learned that other predominantly *straight* churches had been destroyed, too! What a relief, we weren't *singled out!* Other members found themselves still unable to return to church.

An African-American member of my church talked poignantly about how, in the African-American community, church has always been the "safe place." For many African Americans (and for poor folk of different ethnic backgrounds), the church was sometimes the only piece of real estate they ever owned or hoped to own. MCC, like the historic black church, is the "historic" church of the gay and lesbian community. For African Americans, the church was, and sometimes still is, everything; it was where community meetings were held (when they couldn't meet legally in other buildings). It was *theirs;* no one could take it away from them. It was where they discussed voting and politics; it housed the burial societies; it was a place where you could always get help. African-American gays and lesbians at MCC Los Angeles had a different historical perspective, a different lens, perhaps a more intense spiritual and political symbolic investment in the church building than other members. Church structures are not *supposed* to fall down. If *they* fall down, the community is *exposed* and vulnerable in devastating ways.

MCC Los Angeles members who owned their own homes generally did not take the destruction of the church so personally, unless they were African American or had other complicating issues. Thus, the destruction of our building challenged our multicultural community in new ways. We had to communicate more in order to understand each other's particular pains and sorrows.

Latinos and Latinas had yet other concerns. Many of them are immigrants from countries that experience devastating earthquakes, where there was little money for the kinds of seismic preparedness that had been possible in Los Angeles. They had been through experiences where hundreds and even thousands had died in similar earthquakes. They *knew* not to trust the ground. They, of all groups in Los Angeles, took the longest time to reenter their homes, even if they had not had any damage. It took some of the Hispanic members of MCC Los Angeles a very long time to come back to church with any sense of safety, if they ever could. On top of the lack of safety in a culture that is increasingly anti-immigrant, now not even the church was a safe place.

Race, culture, and class privileges made the earthquake less traumatic for some than for others. But even the *most* privileged among us knew that all the retrofitting, all the money and power and education in the world amounted to *nothing* in comparison to the force of this event. For most of us, it was the most powerful external physical force we had ever experienced.

Seismic Sexuality

Life at its core depends on the asymmetry, the messiness, the incompleteness, and the imperfection of the geophysical nature of the planet. What an incredible concept. How are we to understand this theologically? It is as if the planet responds passionately to the asymmetry. In many ways, I think it is interesting to consider this possibility: that volcanoes and earthquakes are, metaphorically speaking, the *sexuality* of the planet. The life urge, the urge to connect, to give birth, to conceive, to change, to grow, to affect and be affected: that is sexuality. That is life.

Are the tectonically unstable and sensitive places or "hot spots" on the planet, like the ring of fire around the Pacific rim, akin to a kind of *erogenous zone* for the planet?

I believe that the third challenge of a mature theology is its capacity to celebrate and embrace sexuality, joy, *embodiedness,* and the big picture.

It is very hard, in our microworlds and with our individualized concerns, to celebrate earthquakes as an expression of the planet's will to *live*, its expression of something like our sexuality. But I do think that's what earthquakes are, metaphorically speaking. Sometimes our human creations and structures do not take the earth and its will to live (a really big picture) into account. Most of the people in Los Angeles who died in the earthquake died in one building that was demonstrated to be unsafe or on freeways that were not as safe as they were thought to be. People also die from earthquakes, floods, and tidal waves where no human ingenuity could have saved them. Sometimes, as small frail life forms, *we are in the way*, in much the same way, perhaps, that the very small life forms that are sometimes in our way are thought to be of no account or worth, and we poison, kill, or sweep them away without a thought.

I am still sometimes haunted by a memory of the aftermath of the Mexico City earthquake in 1985. One of our church members was killed, and others saw death and injuries on a scale from which they have never quite been able to recover. A few days after the quake, we had an ant attack in our kitchen, as happens in Los Angeles when the weather is very dry. The sight of thousands of ants crawling over the kitchen counter repulsed me, as it does many people. I grabbed the bug spray and began to kill them. Suddenly I realized that, for *them,* this was a terrible disaster—a lot like an earthquake or flood, perhaps. I felt helpless and horrible. I did not want to feel this connection *at all.* I wanted to dissociate from these tiny creatures, from any sense of their world or existence. They were in my way. I could so easily regard them as nonlife, to be disposed of at my will, disregarded. I wanted so much *not* to feel it, not to connect them to the human beings in Mexico, to my own humanness, to my own existence and stark vulnerability as a *life form.* It infuriated me that I could not close my mind to these thoughts, and I felt just a little *mad* for a while. I felt grief and shame and helplessness. For a long while, I tried other ant-control methods, some of which I still use, such as keeping little pans of water outside the house, outside doors and windows near their entry points. This seemed to help, at least for a while.

A big picture and a very tiny picture intersected at that moment in a powerful way for me. What about our human desire to control and exploit life—does all life have inalienable rights? When we speak of reverence for life as a value, what kind of life are we talking about? What are the limits, if any? What do I do with all that bug spray? (It is probably bad for the ozone layer anyway!) How far do I have to go in sharing the planet, and with which species?

Quaking In the Bible

There are about 25 references to earthquakes in the Bible. Some of these references are not necessarily *theological* at all, as in this reference from the first verse of the first chapter of Amos:

> The words of Amos, who was among the shepherds of Tekoa, which he saw concerning Israel in the days of King Uzziah of Judah and in the days of King Jeroboam, son of Joash of Israel, two years before the earthquake. (Amos 1:1)

The earthquake: Zechariah mentions the very same earthquake in 14:5, as if all persons reading this will simply know or remember a particular earthquake called "The Earthquake." Anyone alive and near Los Angeles on January 17, 1994, will remember *the* earthquake. Until, of course, something greater in our disaster memory replaces it as a dating device. The earthquake during Amos's lifetime must have had devastating effects to be so singularly remembered. The Oxford Annotated Bible simply comments, "The earthquake, mentioned again in Zechariah 4:5, cannot be precisely dated." Time came when the memory faded and life went on. Sometimes earthquakes, then, are simply recorded as an alternative method of dating a person or events.

There are two categories of the *theological* uses of earthquakes in Scripture. One category I would call earthquakes as *evidence of God's self-expression*. Sometimes earthquakes (accompanied by wind or fire or even sheer silence) are a metaphor for the theophany of God: how God's presence is experienced by humans. This occurs on Mount Sinai (Numbers 16:31–34) and is frequently the case in the Psalms. Earthquakes are also described as the "earth's trembling response to the power of God's presence" (or appearance). This is not the same as the use of earthquakes as an expression of divine wrath—an idea that is alive and well in our times! The book of Revelation is filled with references to violent earthquakes that sometimes kill thousands of people, which is part of an overall apocalyptic vision of the judgment of God upon the wicked. There are hints of this in the "little apocalypses" of Matthew and Luke, including references to earthquakes.

Sometimes just the power and force of the divine, without any particularly negative associations, are viewed as the cause of earthquakes, or earthquakes are interpreted as being motivated by a particular event that has angered God or as signs of God's total, *generic* anger at human beings.

Biblical earthquake theologies don't end here, however; it is even more complicated than that. Earthquakes also seem to play a role in *events related to divine intervention* or that support the divine plan. In one case, an earthquake accompanies Jonathan's (a gay man's?) victory over the Philistines, increasing the "panic in their camp" (1 Samuel, chapters 14 and 15.) In the New Testament, in Matthew's Gospel only, earthquakes accompany both the crucifixion and the resurrection of Jesus. In the account of the resurrection (Matthew 28:2), it is an earthquake that actually rolls the stone away from Jesus' tomb! The *elemental forces* of the universe are called to play a part in this cosmic drama of the death and resurrection of God's anointed. One may wonder if earthquakes were very frequent in those years or if those particular earthquakes would provide dating corroboration for the events. Was this earthquake simply inserted as a literary device meant to heighten the drama of the events or to connect them theologically to God's theophany, God's anger, or to the apocalyptic view of Jesus' life and ministry? Is the mention of earthquakes incidental to those events, or do these events carry more meaning than most scholars have been willing to explore? Are they a part of the backdrop or a component of the events themselves?

Perhaps my favorite earthquake story in the Bible is in Acts 16, the story of Paul and Silas and the jailer.

The book of Acts is the story of the preaching and practicing of the "unhindered Gospel" (Acts 28:31) and the increasing self-discovery of this new movement, which was hardly a church yet. Those early followers of the Way were adventurous, and totally committed to sharing the life-giving, healing grace of God in Jesus Christ. They lived and died to do this.

An earthquake figures in one story of the sharing of the Gospel. Paul and Silas are in Philippi, where they have met Lydia (the seller of purple, you will recall), the women in her prayer group, and, apparently, also some men who are now a part of the church in Lydia's house (Acts 16).

Inevitably, Paul and Silas run into some legal trouble. A slave woman, who the Scriptures say was possessed of a "spirit of divination," was harassing them. Almost offhandedly, Paul, who it says was "very much annoyed" (Acts 16:18), confronts the spirit, and the slave woman is released and in her right mind.

The men who profited from her spiritual or mental illness are not amused. She was a source of income, as people threw coins at this raving psychic. In this story, Christ's messengers align themselves on the side of health and are opposed to those who oppress, dominate, and exploit this slave woman. Paul's and Silas's gift from Jesus of healing is politically and economically *dangerous.* They have rocked the boat. So the merchants have Paul and Silas thrown into jail (without really knowing who they were or that Paul, for instance, is a Roman citizen and should be exempt from such treatment). The story begins this way:

> About midnight Paul and Silas were praying and singing hymns to God, and the prisoners were listening to them. Suddenly there was an earthquake, so violent that the foundations of the prison were shaken; and immediately all the doors were opened and everyone's chains were unfastened. When the jailer woke up and saw the prison doors wide open, he drew his sword and was about to kill himself, since he supposed that the prisoners had escaped. But Paul shouted in a loud voice, "Do not harm yourself, for we are all here." The jailer called for lights, and rushing in, he fell down trembling before Paul and Silas. Then he brought them outside and said, "Sirs, what must I do to be saved?" They answered, "Believe on the Lord Jesus, and you will be saved, you and your household." And the same hour of the night he took them and washed their wounds; then he and his entire family were baptized without delay. He brought them up into the house and set food before them; and he and his entire household rejoiced that he had become a believer in God. (Acts 16:25–34)

Later in the story, the magistrates discover that Paul and Silas are citizens and try to cover up their error. But Paul decides to rub their noses in it a bit. After stopping by Lydia's place to encourage the folks there, they head off again to share the Gospel.

There are some fascinating aspects to this story and to how we might use it to understand its relationship to the issues of sexuality and the church today.

Paul and Silas are singing hymns in jail. The other prisoners, it says, are listening to them—to these two *nuts,* perhaps. Or to some they represent a tremendous sense of hope, strength, and peace that emanates from them. Paul and Silas are no strangers to suffering for the sake of the Gospel. There was joy in enduring suffering for the sake of Jesus, for the sake of a slave girl, now free and in her right mind.

That same spirit I have seen among the South African political detainees, those who were tortured and illegally detained for years in prison for the sake of Jesus. I have seen it in those arrested in AIDS demonstrations, in those arrested in the early days of the civil rights movements, in antiwar protests. They display the joy of suffering for righteousness's sake.

The earthquake was sudden and violent so that the foundations were shaken. In this case, the earthquake, though it is not explicitly stated, functions as an instrument of divine providence. In doing so, the action is sudden and violent. *Shaking the foundations of the prison*—a powerful metaphor for the liberator God. God's action through Christ in these disciples continues to be the same: shaking the foundations of oppression or injustice, of the prisons in which we find ourselves.

One can only imagine how frightening that earthquake was nearly 2,000 years ago—no radio, no Kate Hutton from Cal Tech, and no retrofitting. As the quake subsides, there is shock, a stillness. No one moves apparently. We can wonder whether there is verbal communication among the prisoners, but apparently a decision was made. They decide not to use the earthquake as a reason to run away, to escape. I wonder why not. Might it not seem logical to Paul and Silas that God had provided the earthquake as a means of escape to foil the enemies of God? Instead, they seem to have made the decision to stay for the sake of the jailer. Perhaps there wasn't time for them to escape, or they were unsure if the way was really open.

In any case, the jailer, upon waking and realizing what has happened, simply assumes the worst—that his prisoners have escaped and that he will be killed for allowing them to do so. His fear of what his fate will be is so acute that he plans to kill himself. But, from the dark, there is a voice. How unbelievable that must have seemed to the jailer, like the voice of the gods themselves, the voice of hope and mercy: *"Do not harm yourself, for we are all here."* The jailer is stunned, I presume, by this act of unmerited charity. The prisoners *free* the jailer from his death sentence! He gets his life back in those words. We never actually hear about the other prisoners again. But somehow Paul has managed to be the designated spokesperson and leader. On what basis did he convince the others to stay, one wonders? Did the other prisoners associate the earthquake with the powerful presence of these hymn-singing religious folks? Better do what they tell you, and stay put!

The jailer's whole life and agenda get converted in this story. He no longer seems to care at all what the magistrates do with him. He takes Paul and Silas home with him, feeds them, washes their wounds, and is overjoyed to be associated with them through baptism in Christ. His whole life is turned upside down, and he is grateful! Now he is no longer a prisoner of his *old* life, but a free prisoner of Christ.

I wonder how Paul and Silas knew that the earthquake could be used either as a way to escape or as an opportunity to testify about the love and grace of God in Jesus Christ. What a profound alternative reading, an alternative *earthquake theology* this is! Their own safety, comfort, or vindication is not an issue for them! Everything is about the opportunity to love, to be free, to testify, and to save (the jailer's life and career, this time). There were no guarantees. The jailer could have chosen to kill the prisoners because he could no longer restrain them. He had the only weapon.

In some ways, the prison recalls the tomb of Jesus. I think of the angel announcing to the shocked visitors, "He is not here, he is risen." In almost a play on that story, Paul says, "We are all here." Of course the angel meant Jesus is not here in the tomb. But the point was, Jesus was still *here* but in a new way.

The violent earthquake—crucifixion, disaster—becomes the occasion for new life—Christ's resurrection, this jailer's physical salvation and spiritual conversion.

If, as some churches feel, the issue of homosexuality (sexuality, really) is a *huge seismic fault* that threatens to divide the Christian church at the end of the second millennium, I've been thinking about what a provocative image this is, after all. Is this particular earthquake a disaster, an opportunity, or both? I'm sure the visitors to the tomb that Easter morning at first saw the earthquake as perhaps *one more* disaster (on top of the crucifixion, perhaps another indicator of God's wrath). But instead, of course, it became the method by which the disciples came to know the miracle of the resurrection.

The church is having difficulty seeing the *opportunity* in this seismic debate on human and "homo" sexuality! In many ways, LGBT Christians, imprisoned by the church's outdated and erroneous view about sexual morality, are like Paul and Silas. We might well be expected to use this "earthquake" (the conflict in the church over sexuality) to *escape*, or just pack up and leave. The foundations of the prison are shaking, for God's sake! Can the structures and theology of 2,000 years of Christendom really survive? Do we really want to risk being in the rubble?

But LGBT Christians, like Paul and Silas, know that many nonbelievers are *also* imprisoned by the false theology of the church. The whole culture is permeated with the images and beliefs of a sexually repressed and phobic Christianity. Those who imprisoned Paul and Silas and the others were not the jailer but other more powerful forces "out there." There really was not any escape except to trust God, through their faithfulness, to convert the *entire system* from top to bottom. That's what Paul and Silas thought they were doing, and it is what we need to do!

So they start with the jailer, with the keeper of the tradition, the foot soldier of the power structure, who may have little power in the culture but who does what he is told. Who then are those good church people who keep believing and passing on traditions of condemnation, who are *just doing their jobs,* enforcing the outdated laws of the church? We can only hope and pray that as we are faithful, like Paul and Silas, and *do not run away*, that the experience of our testimony and our faith in God (not the church) will be enough to convert the "jailer." This is because, ultimately, the "secret" will be discovered: that we, LGBT people, are *citizens of the household of faith.* Just like the powers that have realized their error in treating the *citizens* Paul and Silas so rudely, someday the church will have to repent of its treatment of its LGBT *citizens.*

There is also the fate of our *fellow prisoners* in the Christian moral theology jailhouse (tomb) that is both bankrupt *and* corrupt. This theology is bankrupt because it ceases to bring hope, new life, or healing to men and women who suffer terribly not from their sexuality but from how the church *has made them feel or not feel about their embodied selves.* The *least* the church could do, one would hope, is to *do no harm.* But it does great, profound harm.

And I say corrupt. Many closeted LGBT religious authorities harm others in order to protect themselves. They do so because they have what *they believe* to be "dirty secrets," shameful realities about their own sexual lives. Many in church leadership and hierarchies are sick with guilt, shame, and lying. Then they dump this on the rest of us. These are not *only* gays and lesbians but heterosexuals as well: all those who cannot tell the truth about their own sexual histories, lives, or fantasies and who will persecute others who do!

Who are our "fellow prisoners"? They are people who say to me nearly every day, "I'm not religious." This statement is a virtual political necessity in our community. It might be okay or "cool" to be *spiritual*. But it should be a private, highly individual thing, like it used to be! Or it could be very New Age or avant-garde—never *religious*, and certainly not Christian.

When Fr. Malcom Boyd, Rabbi Denise Eger, Rev. LaPaula Turner, and I were arrested during an AIDS protest in front of the Los Angeles County Board of Supervisors, we were taken to our respective county facilities. The men had a much worse time of it than the women did. They were chained to benches and not permitted to go to the bathroom for hours on end.

LaPaula, Denise, and I arrived just in time for lunch, which they served us in the holding cell. I think LaPaula and I were both aware that Denise was a little more of a novice at this than we were. I'd been in jail and had visited lots of people in this particular jail before. We sang songs for her and for ourselves (like Paul and Silas, I guess, though I didn't think of it at the time).

The guards were quiet and low-key, almost not seeing us. We were fingerprinted and kept in the smaller of the holding tanks. Across the aisle, separated by bars and glass, was the holding tank full of women, many of whom looked (to me) to be lesbian. I noticed all of them pointed at LaPaula, Denise, and me. They saw my clergy collar. They were laughing, thinking this was cool: a bunch of preachers busted—for what?

I tried to communicate using the little sign language I knew. I smiled and joked, thinking they knew I was a lesbian. I was able to let them know we were there for an AIDS demonstration. They were all poking each other. They kept laughing until I looked at them and signed something like "I'll pray for you." One woman's face just clouded up, all angry. "Don't pray for me," she signed, folding her arms defiantly. Suddenly, I realized that she thought I meant *praying for her because she was a sinner, a bad person, not like me.* This grieved and hurt me. No, no, I signed. "I'm a lesbian, like you." (I did look around before I said this to make sure no guards would see me.) "Really?" came the response, "No way!" She was all smiles again. "Then you *can* pray for me," she signed. Collar or no collar, I was a *sinner,* just like her.

We at MCC Los Angeles also found this story of Paul and Silas useful, especially in the face of hostile fundamentalist earthquake theologizing about the loss of our building. It became possible to see ourselves as those who could say, "We are still here," after the earthquake! We are not going anywhere; we are still being the people of God in Los Angeles, especially for the gay, lesbian, and bisexual communities, for people with AIDS, for *anyone* who feels judged or excluded from the people of God, especially because of their sexuality. We are still here. Not arson, or persecution, or vandalism, or earthquakes can stop those who know the *real* truth: that we *are* citizens of God's wonderful realm whose ethic is one of unconditional love. We are still here, testifying to jailers, judges, magistrates, and our fellow prisoners. We do not experience things like earthquakes as God's special judgment or favor on anyone but simply as one more marvelous opportunity to share the good news of God's love and to practice that Way in our own city and neighborhood.

When The Prisons Do Not Quake

When I first joined MCC in 1972, I was quite impressed by the fact that MCC from its earliest days had reached out to LGBT folk in jails and prisons: "hard-living" people.[24]

In the late Sixties and early Seventies, "gay" was a new power word and women were just connecting to the word "lesbian." "Homosexual" was the civilized word emerging from psychiatry. We did not have the more middle/upperclass urban image we sometimes have today. We were still considered mostly pretty unmentionable and sleazy, and there were plenty of derogatory labels to go along with the attitudes. Most of us identified with other social outcasts and misfits. We felt brave to find each other—whether in a bar or an MCC church.

We had felt the terrible sting of rejection and the pain of inhospitality, and, in MCC, we were determined, with every breath, not to exclude anyone. We were going to welcome all people into our churches and hearts. We who had been called "sodomites" had been *sodomized* by the church and the culture, and we couldn't bear to do it to anyone else.

In taking this stand, we found ourselves tackling the "sodomite" tendencies of some of the largest institutions in the country: the army, the prisons, the churches, and the hospitals. Places others were trying to get out of, we were trying to get into! We were searching for our people.

As a *class* of people, we gays and lesbians have more familiarity than most with jails and prisons. They form a part of our history. I remember making my first visit to a lesbian bar in the "combat zone" (a street that contained a row of porno theaters, strip joints, and notorious bars) in downtown Boston in the early 1970s and having to run out the back door because a police raid was happening. Every now and then, the police would just rush in the front door of a gay bar and begin rounding everyone up, busting the heads of those who resisted (and the heads of some who didn't). It was during just such a raid that someone said to Troy Perry (in 1968) that surely God *couldn't* love us. It was this statement that propelled Troy into actually holding the first MCC service.[25]

I pastored an MCC church in Worcester, Massachusetts, in the 1970s. After raids at the one gay bar in town (the Ports O'Call on South Main Street), my partner and I would rush to the police station. At the desk there was a TV monitor, where we watched the police beating young adults, even kids in their teens, while dragging them to their cells. We had to keep our mouths shut while we watched or risk getting beaten and jailed ourselves. If that happened, there would have been no one to come for us. So we watched; took badge numbers, times, and dates while desk sergeants grumbled about our presence. Sometimes, if there was a scuffle at the bar or a problem in the making, we would receive a call and race down to the bar trying to intervene before the police arrived. More often than not, the police would just show up for a "surprise visit," and the very sight of them would set off a chain reaction that resulted in arrests and beatings. We then reported these beatings to the Human Rights Commission, who listened empathetically, sometimes even held hearings, and usually did nothing.

While I was pastor of MCC Detroit, we formed a prison ministry team. This included a group of people (mostly lesbians) who began corresponding with inmates in Jackson State Prison, 80 miles from Detroit. Early on in the correspondence, we learned of a lesbian prison inmate in DEHOCO (Detroit House of Correction, a women's state facility that I believe no longer exists) who wanted contact with MCC. I let that information sit on my desk for a few weeks, then finally got around to writing to her. The envelope came back several weeks later, stamped DECEASED. I remember how devastated I felt, holding that unopened envelope in my hands. They had a *pre-printed stamp* saying "DE-CEASED"! This gave me a clue about how often this need for contact had to be communicated to the family and friends of those in prison. I was never able to establish another contact with lesbians in jail or prison while I lived in Detroit.

In 1982, in Los Angeles, a group of women in MCC churches in the area formed a women's prison ministry. We knew no women in prison, although a few members of MCC Los Angeles had actually joined MCC while they were in prison in the 1970s through a jail ministry at Sybil Brand (the Los Angeles women's county jail, which also houses federal prisoners). That ministry and its leaders were no longer around.

Three of us prayed for some kind of opportunity. Two weeks later, the partner of a friend of mine ended up in jail at Sybil Brand. My friend was not amused that I saw this as an answer to prayer! She was much too frightened to have me visit (and thus be identified as a lesbian), but she met a woman who was willing. I think I first visited her the way that family and friends do, standing in line outside sometimes for hours until they call your person's number. Later, I would go through the process of certifying my credentials with the county so that I could visit these women as their pastor, meaning I could bypass the line and meet more privately in the "attorney room." The word spread, and several of us on the team began visiting women on a regular basis, to the dismay of the fundamentalist women's chaplain at Sybil Brand.

We also learned a great deal from the woman who was the president of the group called Friends Outside, an advocacy organization for women in prison: Joyce Ride, mother of Sally Ride. (Her business card actually says, "Mother of the First Woman Astronaut.") Joyce knew all the ins and outs of these places and how to help us deal with an institution that didn't want us to be there.

One of my first encounters was with Yvonne. In her mid-30s, Yvonne, a fairly butch Latina lesbian, had spent most of her adult life bouncing between jail, short stays in prison, and "tours" at Norwalk State Hospital. ("Jail" usually refers to a city or county facility, "prison" to a state or federal institution.) She was an alcoholic, without the possibility of decent long-term treatment.

Yvonne was in jail this time because she was awaiting trial and had no bail money. Yvonne drank at gay bars mostly, but she'd drink at a straight bar if she had to. One night, she did that and went to the trailer park of the man who had been buying her drinks. The trip to his place of residence sobered her up enough so that she realized where she was and what the price was for these drinks. She tried to leave the trailer, and he prevented her (she was about five feet four inches, average size; he was over six feet tall and huge—I saw him myself in court later on). He then tried to rape her, and, in the process, she grabbed a knife from his kitchen and stabbed him.

He lived, but it was awfully close. She was so drunk she remembered nothing of the stabbing or the aftermath.

When I met her, she was in jail, being prosecuted for defending herself. He was out of the hospital and certainly not in jail for attempted rape.

I saw this over and over again: women who were in jail for defending themselves or for harming, even killing, someone who chronically, systematically abused and endangered them.

We bailed Yvonne out and tried to get her into a decent alcoholic treatment program. I failed at the latter. She was not committed enough, probably did not have enough self-esteem to recover, and the opportunity was *not there*. She drank and used. The temporary housing situation I arranged for her disintegrated, of course. One or two nights, she actually slept in my office. One night, after being released from the Glendale City Jail, with her consent, both of us crying, I took her back to Sybil Brand. I felt utterly defeated and enraged. It was the only way I could be sure she would live to testify at the trial. She did live and was sentenced to at least five years in prison.

I visited her in prison but noticed a rapid decline in Yvonne's general and mental health. Years of psychotropic drugs, shock treatments, prescribed medication, alcoholism, and despair had taken their toll. She died before she was 40, before she could complete her sentence. She died of cancer, said the rumor mill. But that's not what killed her.

Eventually, our women's prison ministry established a weekly worship service and chaplaincy program at the California Institute for Women. There I learned the disturbing fact that, for many of the 2,000 women or so warehoused there (in a facility built for 800), prison is the *safest* and in some ways the best place they have ever lived. And it is not a safe or comfortable place. It is prison.

In prison, these women have food and a bed (sometimes in the gymnasium, and without enough toilets). They have the same substandard medical care afforded to all people who are poor in the United States, only their choices are more limited.

I remember the stories of "Doctor No-Touch." He was the only physician who would actually come into one of the state facilities we visited on a regular basis. He was their primary-care physician. Apparently, some time earlier in his illustrious career, this doctor had been accused of improperly touching the women prisoners. His solution (or the state's?) was for him *never to touch the women*. In fact, he stood at least three feet away from them while he spoke to or *examined* them.

Prison doctors come in only two types: those who really also want to be social workers, who are idealistic, and who generally don't last long; and the other kind—the incompetent, negligent, and sadistic. The same can often be said of prison chaplains. As hard as the regimentation is and the various forms of humiliation, there is a kind of community in many of these prisons, especially where women have long stays. Women may be able to form actual friendships. They are not controlled, abused, or exploited by their male family members, partners, friends, or pimps. Lesbians in particular often find themselves in positions of leadership, excelling in an all-female community, not competing with men or having to combat as much homophobia. I saw lesbians who for the first time in their lives felt some self-esteem, some sense of success (in work, in schools, or just socially) in prison in ways they could not feel successful *outside*.

This, of course, is a major cause of recidivism. I met women who committed crimes in order to get back into prison to be with lovers or friends. These women, when they left prison, were leaving the only home they had ever known to be anything remotely like a home, where there was some safety from violence (not totally, by any means), lots of rules (boundaries), a pretty clear system of rewards and punishments, and the possibility of intimacy. For most of these women, leaving was like trying to catch a speeding train, like leaving home without a safe place to go. One solution would be to make prison more unattractive, less safe, as many have suggested. How *bad* would it have to be, I wonder, to be less safe than the *outside*?

It was really hard for me to take in this lesson: that prison, with the boredom, the regimentation, the arbitrariness of the discipline at times, the negligent medical care, the bad food, the limited opportunities

(women get much less of the percentage of funds for job training, reha-
bilitation, and education in the California prison system than do men),
the overcrowding, the shame attached, the fact that they often lost their
children—even with all this, prison was an *improvement* in their lives! For
some, it was the only positive attention and support they ever got from *anyone* in authority; the only real education that they got.

Over and over again, as we prepared to welcome women and to be a
part of their "program" as they tried to reestablish a life outside of prison
and outside of the environment that had led them to prison in the first
place, we ran into this. They were lonely and afraid, and it took money
and volunteers to help them make it on the outside. Some had babies or
children to care for as soon as they got out, had no place to live, and only
200 dollars. Usually, if they made it past the first two weeks, I began to
have a little hope. I watched them try, and try hard, and then give up
and go back. They'd go back exhausted and defeated.

The lesbian lifers always fascinated me. The ones I met, of course,
were a select group—those who were motivated to come and be part of a
lesbian-identified church in the place they might very well spend the rest
of their lives. These women did not come primarily because I could help
them when they got out. They were there to make life better on the inside
for themselves and others. There was a kind of freedom among the lifers.
Somehow, this boundary of time and space helped them relax. They had
a place finally to be who they were, in a fundamental sense. This final,
very hard reality of lifelong imprisonment freed them in a way. They were
the ones who gave MCC inside the walls the name "Free-Spirit MCC."

Some of these women were very admired by the others and given affectionate nicknames. They were available for spiritual and emotional support to the other women. They oriented them. They were the ones the
others looked to, to see if they thought we from MCC on the outside were
okay. We had to prove ourselves to these women first. They also always dis-
played to me this tremendous kindness and openness.

Who Preaches in Prisons?

Protestant religious ministries in jails and prisons do tend to be dominated by fundamentalists. They are our primary "competition" for the
women's hearts and minds. This, I believe, is true for several reasons. For
the most part, mainline Protestants have simply written off people in jail

or prison—for class reasons primarily and because their racial group (white) is underrepresented among prison populations. More poor and working-class people and people of color (even if they now have jobs and money) have relatives or friends who are or have been in jail or prison. Therefore, the churches that reach out to and serve those ethnic groups and classes will tend to be involved in jail and prison work.

This became especially apparent to me after I began pastoring at MCC Los Angeles. Our church was about 40 percent people of color. On an average of at least once a week, I heard about family members or close friends who get shot, stabbed, raped, or sent to jail or prison, who are returning from jail or prison, who are getting out of the hospital from a gang fight, or who get killed in a drive-by shooting. I would guess that 95 *percent* of the time it was people of color who told me these stories.

Members of our congregation who love each other and try to work together, especially in the LGBT community, *live* and sometimes *work* in different worlds, with different dangers and pressures. Sometimes it's like we live in different cities that only occasionally (like during the riots or earthquakes) get to touch or see each other.

Because political conservatism or an "apolitical" stance (the same thing!) makes these religious groups less threatening to the status quo of the criminal justice system (especially jails and prisons), fundamentalists are much more welcome in such institutions by the authorities. They are less likely to question either the prison's rules or the officials themselves, and, in a sense, are seen as working hand in hand with the institution to control the prisoners.

Finally, fundamentalist theology is also well suited to this purpose. It works entirely on an individualistic framework. The focus is on the individual's sinfulness and the need for salvation. It feeds on guilt and shame and seeks to help the person control himself or herself, using the fear of eternal punishment and the desire for eternal reward. It is well suited to the prison context and philosophy. It has simple, straightforward answers for someone whose life is in ruins, who feels desperate, lost, and hopeless. It also helps a person to stop focusing on the frustrations of this life, of present circumstances, or on individual experiences of injustice or oppression. It's all the prisoners' fault, and God will forgive them (if they behave from now on and keep quiet), and things will improve in the *next* life. Nothing else is important.

What happens to LGBT people in jail or prison is that they are not only losers in this life but they are told they are losers in the next life as well! They are often harangued from the pulpits of these institutions as the worst of sinners. The fundamentalists (and Catholics, secondarily) are practically given a franchise on prison ministries and are free to preach their homophobic gospel without interference from the government, which builds and maintains these institutions with our tax money (including LGBT tax money). Some of the ministries are privately funded, but there are state-funded chaplaincies that are sometimes extremely homophobic.

One major exception to this practice was the presence of a paid (by the state) MCC chaplain at Vacaville, California—because they had so many prisoners with AIDS and HIV, and MCC clergy have had more experience with AIDS than anyone else. Our presence at Vacaville was a profound breakthrough.

Every time MCC goes into a prison, we have had a fight on our hands. If it does not come from the institution itself (only because we have already fought them in court and won), we face harassment and opposition from the fundamentalist chaplains who work there and who cooperate with prison officials. They want no one visiting prisoners who are going to inform them of their rights; to challenge the institution's rules, policies, or practices in any way; or to challenge their homophobic theology and biblical interpretation. In all fairness to the front-line prison officials and guards, it is sometimes not too hard to understand why. Underfunding of basic services and overcrowding create a constant state of emergency that is dangerous and difficult for everyone. When people like us come along, all they can see is trouble.

At one institution, the sequence was as follows: a group of women wrote to me saying they wanted MCC services at a state women's prison. I contacted the chaplain and had a conference with him. I reminded him of the fact that we had sued the state of California some ten years before and had won the right to visit our parishioners and hold worship services for them in state prisons, like any other church. He then tried to debate with me about homosexuality and the Bible. I gave him our materials and said it really wasn't important to me whether or not he agreed with us, but we wanted to hold these services.

He agreed and gave us Thursday nights twice a month. We went and met these women for the first time. The crowd was a little smaller than anticipated, and then I realized that they were "letting" us use the administration room, which required that everyone attending had to sign a register before entering this part of the facility! This meant *coming out* in writing to the institution. Nevertheless, some women braved this and came anyway. This took remarkable courage. I felt embarrassed that they were forced to go through this just to meet with us for the first time. In subsequent weeks, the numbers grew. Gradually, the women became less afraid.

We were clear that all women (not just lesbians) were welcome, and some straight friends came as well. Then we ran into other problems. We would arrive, and they would say that there had been a "problem" inside, they were doing a *count* (of prison population), and we would not be able to get in until 8:00 in the evening (we were usually there at 6:30, and the prison was an 80-mile drive from the church).

So we would say, "Fine, we'll be back at 8:00." We knew they expected us just to leave. But we didn't. We went away and came back. This meant that we would not leave until nearly 10:00, and still had to drive 80 miles home. When we did return, often only a few women were there to greet us. They weren't sure whether we had just not shown up, or had been delayed, or, if we had been there, whether we were coming back. It took a long time for them really to trust that we'd be that committed. Sometimes, it was obvious that they had been waiting for us *all that time*—that we had been lied to. Other times, we almost got the feeling the prison official had scheduled this extra count just to interfere with our program. This happened nearly every other time we came, and it was meant to discourage us and the women inside. Instead, it made us more determined.

Finally we were able to get out of the administration building into a classroom on the inside, where no one had to sign in and go through security to come to our services. Then they changed the prison recreation schedule and made Thursday night softball practice and shopping night! Women worked together to shop for each other so they could take turns coming to church, but "competition" with the softball practice was too hard for us to overcome, and our attendance suffered again. We petitioned for another night or even a weekend time but were turned down.

Only when the fundamentalist chaplain was hospitalized for an extended time did we get a break. The Catholic chaplain was more relaxed and empathetic. We asked him for a weekly meeting time on the weekend with the ability to use the chapel, and we got it all. Six years later, we were still meeting every Saturday in that chapel.

But the harassment didn't stop. Many times, our ministers and volunteers would arrive at the prison to find that their names had not been left at the desk and "cleared," even though we had sent the officials a list in writing and had called and double-checked during the week. When we would arrive at the desk, as we did every week, and try to get in, we would be denied. There was no avenue for appeal, and many times women would be waiting for us at the chapel and we could not get in. Meeting with prison officials and chaplains would clear the problem for a month or two, and then it would start all over again.

But the women still came, and they waited for us. They waited for women who were lesbians like them, who preached about a God of compassion and justice, who understood their sorrows, their feelings, their goals, their hopes and fears. They wanted to hear about a God who had not forgotten them and who was not judging them for being who they were—a God who wanted them to know they were loved just the way they were. What we hoped to accomplish was that, in meeting MCC clergy-women and lay volunteers, the women would have *enough* of an experience of MCC that when they got out they could come to an MCC service and feel at home, feel a connection that could help them make the transition to the outside.

Sometimes, we even arranged it so that one or two MCC lesbians or friends would be right there to greet the women as they were released and bring them to a Sunday morning service right from the prison itself. (We even encouraged them to petition for Sunday morning release, even if that meant staying an extra day or two.) They would then see the clergy and lesbian volunteers they had come to know and trust just a little bit. We then often had to help with the difficult issues of temporary housing, job search, child care, and readjustment. Sometimes, we would actually be successful, and there are women who have been able to leave prison behind permanently. Finally, it was *not* the best place they'd ever been.

Kenneth was 17 when he entered Jackson State Prison in Michigan, a poor, biracial, effeminate gay man (adolescent). He had killed someone in a drug- and gang-related context. He was still in the first few years of his life sentence when I met him. He was the first gay prisoner who ever wrote to me. Somehow, he had gotten hold of a regional gay publication that had mentioned me and MCC Detroit.

I knew Kenneth for nine years. Then they moved him to another prison, and I lost track of him, I'm sorry to say.

It was so hard to believe. This bright, engaging, spiritual young man, his life trashed so early by a tragic series of events. Not that Kenneth ever *pretended* to be innocent or anything other than who and what he was. He was refreshingly honest. Almost instantly, he grasped the message of MCC, *a church for all people with a special outreach to the gay and lesbian community*. Behind the stale walls of Jackson State Prison, he breathed us in, our willingness to know him, to love him and his friends. He knew his cellmates and fellow gay prisoners needed a nonjudgmental, inclusive, compassionate perspective on the Bible and homosexuality, on God and the church of Jesus Christ. He was a leader, handsome, energetic, and passionate about what he believed.

Kenneth always talked nonstop when we met. He was an organizer, and the prison hated that. But he was smart and overly polite; sometimes, he reminded me of a black drag queen version of Eddie Haskell, from the 1950s television show *Leave It to Beaver*. He *really* irritated the authorities and entertained us! He knew how to get things done. He got as many as 80 or 90 prisoners to sign a petition to have MCC come inside the walls of Jackson State Prison. He didn't discriminate either—he talked his Muslim friends into signing as well! We would coach Kenneth at our bimonthly meetings, fitting in lessons about homosexuality and the Bible, teaching about MCC and our beliefs. He would take these back inside and weekly send us more names of people to visit while we were there. Our trip to Jackson got more involved; four or five of us would go and spend a whole Saturday visiting these gay men. Mostly lesbians went on these excursions. There we were, four or five white lesbians visiting mostly men of color who were also gay.

That confused the authorities at the prison terribly. *They couldn't figure it out.* What was this all about? Why were we visiting these men? What were our perverted or sinister motives? Somehow, they just didn't buy the church thing. We must be on some kind of weird sex trip. They could never believe that we believed we had anything in common with these guys—many of them "dangerous criminals."

They could never believe that to us these men were brothers— brothers in Christ and gay brothers. We saw ourselves in them. We saw in their prisons our own prisons; we saw their real and coming freedom as our freedom too. We had a common foe as well—a ruthless symbol of the racism and homophobia that kill and ruin so many lives: Jackson State Prison, which prides itself on being the "largest walled prison in the world."

Every week, we were fighting the officials, the fundamentalist chaplains, the guards, and the terrible self-images of these men, their despair, their grief, and their fears. We touched them when permitted, we prayed for them, and we even eventually found homes for some of them who made it out. Mostly, we told them over and over again that God did not hate them or us for being gay and that their lives had meaning, purpose, and value to us and to God. Sometimes, I think we should have prayed for an earthquake!

They petitioned to hold worship services in the prison, and the request was denied. Having won a similar suit in the state of California just two years before, we felt very excited about our prospects. Meanwhile, we kept up our visitation schedule and correspondence with these men. We also petitioned for the right to serve them Holy Communion, and were again denied.

We spent nine years and thousands of dollars in state and federal court while the state stuck to its story that we couldn't hold these services because the inmates who wanted to attend would be endangered. The state did not think it should be required to *prove* that abridging their constitutional right to freedom of religion was necessitated for security reasons. None of the 80 or so gay men who asked for those services believed that the other men would attempt to hurt them if they went to MCC services. But the state insisted that the reason it wanted to keep us out was for the safety of the prisoners, gay or straight, who wanted to attend MCC. We even argued that, if they thought there would be a problem, why didn't they put on a few extra guards and just test out their theory for a few weeks?

We lost our final appeal in federal court, which supported the prison's claim that the anticipated "violence" that would occur if MCC held services there was enough of a reason to keep us out—violence that none of the petitioners anticipated or were afraid of facing.

By the time the last appeal was heard nine years later, I had left MCC Detroit and was working for MCC in California. The appeals court did rule that we could serve communion, under close scrutiny, to five prisoners at a time in a small office just off the visiting room. The last time I saw Kenneth was in that room. For the first and only time in Jackson State Prison, I consecrated communion with these men, and we shared communion MCC style. Two of the men had never received communion in their lives. Kenneth had been Catholic, and the other man was Baptist. So I explained communion first, then consecrated. I asked Kenneth to serve me, and that was almost too much for him. I remember how his voice broke and his hands shook as he served me. Nine years he had devoted to this moment, this small victory, this holiest of communions. I left to catch my plane to California, but I will always feel like I left a part of my heart in that room.

Kenneth would hold small meetings of MCC on the yard, in the dining area, wherever the men could congregate and converse unmolested. He read the MCC bylaws carefully and noticed that we ask each church to take an offering each Sunday and forward 10 percent to the headquarters. Kenneth took this obligation very seriously and was deeply troubled because the men were not permitted to carry cash on their person or to send cash anywhere. So we worked out a compromise that he suggested. A lot of the men whom Kenneth evangelized were drag queens, only some of whom could manage to buy or get hold of makeup (I have no idea how). And for the "butch" guys, cigarettes were always in demand. So Kenneth took up collections of makeup and cigarettes, which he distributed to the less fortunate among them and even managed to get to those who were in solitary confinement. Sometimes, the collections were so generous he hardly had space in his cell to hide it all! He was still bothered occasionally by the dilemma of how to tithe 10 percent to headquarters, but we just kept telling him that he was doing the right thing and that they were a wonderful example. Theirs was a powerful new twist on Jesus' story of the "widow's mite": two cigarettes and half a used lipstick—a powerful illustration of the doxology sung in so many churches every Sunday:

"We give Thee but Thine own, what e'er the gift may be.
All that we have is Thine alone, a trust, O Lord, from Thee."

4 • Equal to Angels

On a trip to visit friends in Los Angeles with my wife Paula and her mother, Paula's mother was relating the latest homophobic comment she had heard in her small Michigan hometown. One of Paula's now ancient elementary school teachers is a member of Paula's mother's church. Somehow, the subject of *those people* came up, and "Mrs. Smith" (not her real name!) said, "Well, they're all heathens, you know!" Paula's mother said it made her speechless. Her daughter a *heathen?* What does this term mean in this day and age? What images does that evoke? Words like *heathen* and *pagan* evoke racist, sexist images—white, male, oppressive Christian missionary stereotypes. This is more than ignorance; it's more mean-spirited than that. LGBT people are sort of the ultimate *other* lurking heathenishly by schoolyards, or in public rest rooms, or sleazy bars, or ... you can fill in the blank. So our demonized public image made me think again about the possibility of gay and lesbian angels.

I want to make it clear that I am not saying that all gay and lesbian people are angels or angelic. What I am trying to suggest is that there are powerful biblical correctives to the demonized view of queer folk.

We LGBT people need to see ourselves and be seen as *fully human,* neither as angels nor demons. I remember when we asked the World Council of Churches on behalf of MCC to *consider* including LGBT people (who are executed and tortured in many countries just for being *suspected* of being gay) in their human rights agenda. We weren't even asking them to support *civil rights* for LGBT people, or to provide religious validation. We were just asking them to support *human* rights: meaning the right not to be imprisoned, tortured, exiled, or murdered simply for being homosexual. When they hesitated, hemming and hawing, whining that this was "bad timing" for the WCC (never mind the "bad timing" for those being abused and murdered!), I realized the depth of the problem once again: they're not sure we're human! Human rights seemed to them to be an unreasonable request *at this time.*

Recently, Janice, a lesbian I know, was a participant in a support group for women of her culture and race who were surviving with breast cancer. She was very out of the closet in her personal and professional life, but, in the few weeks she'd been attending, the subject of sexuality or partners had not come up. Two days before Janice's surgery, a woman in the group challenged Janice about the fact that she is lesbian and said, "I can't support you in this group if you are a lesbian." Janice was hurt, speechless, never dreaming that this would be a problem. She never returned to the support group. Being a woman of color and trying to stay alive with breast cancer was *not enough* to bring solidarity, to overcome homophobia! It was okay with this woman to turn Janice out, to cause her stress two days before surgery, for her to live *or* die without human support from other *sisters.* How do we unmask this kind of violence?

In some ways the concepts of "angels" and "demons" are constructions of a perceived split in the human moral and spiritual self—the good and bad in all of us. On the other hand, the Bible and a lot of Christian (and non-Christian) theology have posited *actual beings* in a spiritual realm, known as demons or angels. There has been a virtual fad in recent years of speculating about the existence of such angelic beings.

We probably get more of our ideas about angels from popular culture (Clarence the bumbling angel in *It's a Wonderful Life,* for instance) than from the Bible. In the Bible, angels are often fierce, frightening, or so well disguised that they are able to pose as ordinary humans, like the angels in Genesis 19.

What I am interested in is the process of *suggestion* and *association,* not necessarily a thoroughgoing theology of angels. In Los Angeles (the city of angels), one of the AIDS service agencies, the one that provides lunches to housebound people with AIDS, is called Project Angel Food. To those who are lying in beds of pain and weakness (sometimes with no one to visit or stay with them during the day), a person appearing at their door with a smile and a hot meal *is* an angel.

LGBT people were the ones who started most of the AIDS agencies in the United States, and in other countries, during the first decade of the AIDS epidemic. Those organizations were built and are sustained by hundreds of thousands of volunteers and volunteer hours. One of the sociological realities that has made this possible is that proportionately fewer LGBT people are encumbered with the demands of child care and raising children (though that is changing!). But even those who *do* have children were swept into the tremendous community effort that cared for hundreds of thousands of ill and dying friends, lovers, neighbors, and strangers. Armies of LGBT angels and Mother Teresas feed, clothe, bathe, nurse, hold, hug, touch, carry, and love the sick and dying men, women, and children who have AIDS. It's not that straight people have not also been there, done it— but, especially in the early days, we did *most* of it. And we've also done the praying, the memorials and funerals (sometimes when no one else would do them), and the comforting. We've done this in the face of the virulent, religiously motivated homophobia and AIDS phobia that communicate to the world, "AIDS is God's gift to the gay community."

The need has become overwhelming, and many LGBT persons with any leisure time or disposable income have been pressed into service or extra giving in some way for some period of time. For those of us in MCC, AIDS has dominated our local church pastoral care services and our community outreach programs for decades.

Everyone who serves selflessly in our culture is deemed an "angel" in the popular mind. The term *angel,* as in "be an angel," has come simply to mean someone who will serve another not for selfish gain and who does it cheerfully, without being expected to be paid back. Somehow, deeds of kindness and charity are beyond what we think we can reasonably expect of other humans. Somehow, "be a human" doesn't conjure up the same warm, openhearted, giving image!

In fact, "I'm only human" is the great excuse for letting ourselves and others down. It is the all-encompassing excuse for screwing up. What a definition of humanness!

Sometimes, the concept of angels is linked to those who have died, as a description of their afterlife role. I have not found a particular biblical justification for this point of view. Mostly, the Bible seems to view angels as a separate category of existence. Angels are a special species of spiritual beings, independent of humans: they are messengers from God who communicate with us from time to time but who mostly seem busy keeping God company in heaven.

Nevertheless, this popular version of the afterlife has humans living a quasi-angelic existence and sometimes includes the assumption that after death we get transformed (or recycled) as angels. It's not clear to me if this includes all people, even ordinary people (like the seemingly inept Clarence from *It's a Wonderful Life)*, or only *really, really good* people. Also, the relationship of angelic existence to what the church has called the "communion of saints" is not very clear. However, popular theology does not worry itself about theological *correctness!*

The concept of the communion of saints in Christian theology is the belief that those who die *in Christ* commune together eternally before the throne of God and that, from time to time, the church experiences their collective witness and presence (Hebrews 12). We might say that this is the way in which Westerners incorporate the ancient (and, in indigenous cultures, nearly pervasive) practice of venerating (or worshiping or honoring) one's ancestors.

In fact, I remember the story of a young man in Germany who was the partner of the German-born pastor of MCC Hamburg. This young man had been a "boat person," a refugee from Vietnam. At age 11, he was rescued by Australians and eventually sent by church people to Germany, where he was placed in a foster home. John was gay. A Vietnamese gay man, he was now a German immigrant. His religion of origin was a Vietnamese native religion that was based on ancestor worship. He attended one of his first Christian worship services ever in London at an MCC European conference. There, at an AIDS vigil, he heard people calling out the names of those who had died of AIDS, praying for them and their families and friends, naming and mourning the losses. John, for whom English is a third language, was not sure what was happening. He whispered to his partner, a former Baptist pastor, "Are they calling on their ancestors?" It was a very logical and reasonable assumption! Also, there was *truth* in that question. Hebrews 11 speaks of our "ancestors in faith" and what it means to remember those who die in faith as part of a heavenly community. Many of those who have died of AIDS are our *spiritual ancestors,* our particular communion of saints.

One of the things that has happened to LGBT people because of AIDS and because of the virtual epidemic of breast cancer among women in the United States and among lesbians is that we have had to experience the death of dozens or even hundreds or thousands of people we have known personally or have known of, who were often our own ages, more or less. We are experiencing this *selective holocaust* while the rest of the world goes on with business as usual (meaning the usual, expected, and also horrific losses—car accidents, other illnesses, etc.). There are times when I have greeted my friends and colleagues at MCC meetings, and we have spent the first five minutes saying, in small talk, not "How are you?" but a litany of "Did you hear? Did you know that James died, that Ginny is in the hospital, that Al is not expected to live the week?" People whose deaths would have had a big impact on my life ten years ago sometimes— terribly, tragically—become a footnote in my day, as in "By the way, Bob died (yesterday, last week, did I forget to tell you?)."

In December 1993, we had a very long staff meeting at MCC Los Angeles. At the end of the meeting, we were making prayer requests. I asked for prayers for our young assistant pastor, Dan Mahoney, who was dying of AIDS, and for a young colleague, a student clergy, Doug, who had been in a class I had taught. I mentioned that I was going to visit Doug in the hospital the next morning. My associate pastor, Lori, turned to me, put her hand on my arm, and said quietly, "Doug died this morning." I remember the shock wave—like a little electrical jolt—that went through me. She thought I knew already. I didn't. Now I did. And there was the *terrible* thought that was *partially* a relief: one less hospital visit to make— then guilt. I was too late: he had left without my visit. How is his partner Bruce doing? I filed those questions in my mind and went home.

The next day, I went to the Veterans Administration Hospital business office with my assistant pastor's partner, Patrick, trying to cut through red tape to get Dan into a hospice. This took nearly three hours. While I was at the hospital, my father died. I flew into my office as usual, and a volunteer said, "Your mother has called twice; she's holding on line one for you now." My mother *never* calls me at my office. I knew before I answered the phone.

While I was in New York at my father's funeral, Dan Mahoney died. He had been my assistant pastor *and* dear friend for many years. At his funeral, I learned of the death of two other people whom I knew and of the critical illness of another. Sometime later that month, I realized that Doug's funeral had been held the same day as my dad's. It seemed finally to have happened to me—what had happened to so many of us: the body count got too high, the pile too deep. I had lost track, I couldn't keep up,

I kept meaning to call Doug's partner, Bruce; I think I left a message on his machine; I'm not sure I ever did. Three months later, I managed to go over to him and hug him at the funeral of a mutual friend's father. The circle closed for a moment—but only for a moment.

The lines between life and death blur in this process. The less-than totally reliable rumor mill sometimes has people dead and buried before they're hospitalized! Or it leaves others behind, pitifully long dead before anyone has time to notice. Sometimes, when people get ill, they shut out their friends and church family. The hardest days for some of us are finally getting through to someone who tells us, "Santiago died three months ago; didn't you know?"

Lloyd was an angel; I'm sure of it. I met him through fellow angel Lew. Lew ended up at a different hospital than he usually went to, and afterward I would come to believe that it was so I could meet Lloyd.

On the AIDS ward that day at this hospital, there were a number of patients in need. Also, as usual, I was already running behind schedule, which meant I was not feeling as relaxed and attentive as I would like to be while visiting people in the hospital. I finally got *out of there* and was rushing through the lobby to the parking lot when a woman stopped me.

I must digress for a moment. Being a clergywoman and wearing a clerical collar in public is always an interesting experience—especially in lobbies, on lines, or in elevators, where someone feels compelled to make conversation. Once, in an elevator at the Veterans Administration Hospital, a young, tall, pleasant-looking man said, "Are you a minister?" (That, by the way, is the most common question. I'm not sure that any clergyman in a clerical collar has ever been asked that question.) Over the years I've tried to think of clever comebacks, but none of them quite matches the strangeness of the question. I think I always want to ask them why they think anyone would wear this silly outfit if she or he were *not* a clergyperson? What is it they imagine I'm doing in this shirt if I'm *not* a clergyperson? Anyway, sometimes, "Are you a minister/priest/clergyperson?" is the whole of the matter. But this day it also included *"because . . . "* (uh-oh, here we go!). At this point, the young man looked furtively around in the empty elevator while also assessing just how many floors we had left in which to continue this conversation: "because the doctors want me to give them a sperm sample to take a test, and they want me to, you know, touch myself to get the sample. I thought maybe there was *another way to get it.*"

Now, as a frequent victim of people's sexual projections and unique and interesting forms of sexual harassment, I can pretty much tell *which* kinds of conversations are going in *what* directions with *what* motives. Even though I might have *preferred* this question to be the garden-variety sexual come-on or harassment (a new variation on an old theme), I had the sinking feeling that he was absolutely sincere. It is strange to think that I might have preferred it to be harassment—but that's probably because then I could have just confronted it or brushed it off. I also recognized that he was developmentally disabled in some way, though this was not immediately apparent. I replied, "So, you were taught that masturbation is a sin, and the problem is that these doctors are asking you to do something you were taught was wrong?"

"Yes," he said, relieved that I had understood him and said some words he couldn't quite say. Somehow, in the next few seconds, I was able to ask him if this test was really necessary and important. He said, "Yes." I asked him to consider whether he could let himself think about how God had created and loved him. Could he perhaps think that God would make an exception in this case because of his health and that God would not be angry at him if he masturbated for a really good reason? At this he broke into a smile and said, "Yes, ma'am, thank you!" At that, he ran off the elevator.

Sadly, there was no time to talk to him about God and guilt and sexuality and all that good stuff of contemporary sexual and ethical discourse! And I didn't want to give him just my answer. But he needed permission to think of God (and his own body) differently for the moment and to try on an alternative answer. It was a strange momentary dilemma for me. At that moment, to him, I had the authority to speak for God, as a clergyperson (perhaps a lesser type of angel) to whom he could ask a very private, vulnerable question in the confines of our temporary elevator/confessional. He related to me with a touching, childlike innocence and trust, not worrying that I would be offended, or shocked, or put off, and I guess I wasn't. I took him seriously, at his word. And I knew he simply needed to be released from a false sexual guilt, from a terrible legalistic burden: forced to choose between health and God's approval.

I've had hundreds of encounters like these, some even more "high risk." Being female and lesbian, I've probably had more than most. Women are great, wonderful, when they see me in my collar: they get excited and curious. On one airplane trip, a Baptist flight attendant couldn't stop looking at me or talking to me. She wouldn't let me get back to reading my book. Women who have always wanted a woman pastor but have never seen one before often want to confide in me or to touch me, to take me home with them, and replace their male pastor with me.

Ralph was an HIV-positive member of my church. His 70-year old mother, a gospel singer in ministry with her husband for *50 years,* was getting divorced. (The husband had run off with a younger female choir member.) She was devastated, and her church family shunned her, and her male pastor *blamed* her. For some, divorce is always the woman's fault. Her shame and rage were overwhelming her, as well as her vulnerability—ashamed and divorced at age 70, with a son who was vulnerable, too. We talked for hours. She was embarrassed that she had always teased Ralph about going to *that church!* (meaning that awful gay church.) She loved being able to talk to a woman pastor, *forgetting* that I was a lesbian from *that church!*

While attending a Roman Catholic seminary, I took a class with a group of older Catholic sisters, none of whom had ever even had a chance to go to college. The course was on prayer and included self-esteem as part of the subject matter discussed. Sister Dorothy complained that, in all these years in the convent, she was supposed to *obliterate* any thoughts of self, and now she was expected to account for her level of self-esteem! I fell in love with these women. And they doted on me, which simply increased my infatuation. They were so excited that I was a clergywoman. They wanted to know about my sermons, what I wore; they touched me before and after every class.

Then they invited me to lunch after class one day. They wanted to hear *all* about my church and ministry. All my internalized homophobia got stimulated. Somehow, in some corner of my self-esteem, I had come to rely on these women, their approval, and their support. Would it continue if they knew I was a lesbian? But I couldn't dodge them or their questions anymore. So I told them first about MCC (then later about me!). When I told them of our LGBT outreach, Sister Elisabeth got quiet and said to Sister Dorothy, "But we were always taught that homosexuality was wrong, Sister!"

Sister Dorothy rushed to my defense, saying, "Listen, they lied to us about a lot of things, Sister: remember that self-esteem business?" Right on, Sister Dorothy. They *did* lie to us a lot, especially about our bodies, about being female or gay. The night the sisters came and visited me at MCC Detroit was a special treat, a memory to treasure. The Catholics at MCC Detroit that night were a little traumatized at first to see eight nuns—in their habits—troop into the second row of pews in our sanctuary: they thought they were having a horrible *lapsed-Catholic nightmare*. But, by the end of the evening, everyone had calmed down. As an extra bonus, seeing Sister Dorothy take communion from *me* healed a lot of doubt in a lot of formerly Catholic MCCers that night.

Back to Lloyd's story. I was in the lobby, rushing as usual, dressed in my suit and clergy collar, when Lloyd's sister stopped me. Now, when I am in a hurry, you have to be very quick and determined to stop me, and she was. She grabbed my arm, in fact, and said, "What kind of clergy are you? I mean," she amended, "what kind of church are you from?"

Well, I looked at her. It was just possible that she was a lesbian. She had spotted me. So I cut to the chase; "I'm with MCC."

She grinned, "I thought so! My brother is upstairs having surgery right now. He has AIDS, and he's having a hard time. Will you see him?" I said yes, got the details, and went back the next day. (My friend Lew, by the way, was then transferred to another hospital or went home that day, his angelic mission accomplished!)

Lloyd was a little guy, strawberry blond, just like his lesbian sister (my gaydar had been right!), with a sweet Southern Illinois/Kentucky country accent. He poured out his heart about dying, about all his worries (ex-partners and family members, gay and straight, leaned on him a lot). And his business (a West Hollywood drugstore) was really like a ministry to Lloyd. He loved his customers: they were more like clients or parishioners. He felt too needed, too responsible, to die.

Something happened to me when I met Lloyd. For about two years previously, I had been nearly unable to cry at all. I might tear up a little, but I could not cry and certainly could not weep, even by myself. I was shut down, with all the compounded grief and anger. The part that could just spontaneously weep or tear up (which had never ever been easy for me anyway) was totally locked away. As I sat with Lloyd, this gentle, little stranger, I held his hand. He began to sob quietly, and the sight of him made me cry. The pleasure of those tears (fogging my glasses, wetting my cheeks) was enormous. My crying did not disturb him: it seemed to help him feel not so alone. Together we cried for so many things, including ourselves.

Every time Lloyd went into the hospital, I would see him. And I would hear a little more about this man's life. After crying with him, I cried every day that week, in my car, at home. It became natural and easy to tear up in my office, at hospices and hospitals, even when I spoke or preached. I felt like I had been healed of a disability. Lloyd had helped me in that moment to reopen to my own tears.

We held his memorial service at the juice bar next door to his drugstore. The place was packed with family, friends, and customers. A big poster-size picture of Lloyd in a happier, healthier time dominated the room. Over and over, people testified to Lloyd's kindness and generosity—how much he gave and gave away, how he saved their lives, their dignity. They described how he was more than a druggist—he was a friend, a healer, and a brother. Lloyd is a part of my own communion of saints. Sometimes, having lost count a long time ago, I wonder if I know more people who have died than I know ones who are *presently alive*. Sometimes, the line between the world of the living and the alive and the world of the dying and the dead is very blurred for me—as if I, like so many in my community now, live in that strange borderland between the living and the dead, where people are continually crossing over. It is a mysterious and awesome place to live. You learn how true it is that death is not a moment but a series of moments, a process. And everyone does it his or her own way. I have sat by the dead bodies of young dear friends, women and men, holding their still-warm, gradually cooling hands. I have watched their strained and pain-lined faces relax. Miraculously, tenderly, they have seemed to grow younger in that twilight moment of release.

It is a great privilege to accompany them to their border crossing. It is also not what I expected to be doing in the fourth and fifth decades of my life. And I was so enraged and overwhelmed at times that I wanted to find *someone* to blame: I wanted revenge. I wanted someone to pay for all this needless suffering, including, I guess, my own. Who pays for all this stolen life and stolen time, including my life and time? And then I thought of the arrogance of that thought, that complaint. Who guarantees anyone one minute of life? Where did I get off feeling *ripped* off—especially when I've had the privilege of loving and serving the dying?

I'm not the only one, I've discovered, who has been profoundly, eternally impacted by the untimely death of dozens, even hundreds of friends,

colleagues, and acquaintances. Other friends and colleagues reported seeing people in public who they were sure, for an instant or longer, were
friends who had long since died. Now and then I would have a powerful
sensory memory of someone and then check the date: it's their birthday
or the anniversary of their death.

Jean Foye was a very *human* angel. A lifelong alcoholic with "bouts" of sobriety, she knew everyone, especially Hollywood old-timers. One day, she wan-
dered sullenly into the church. She was a raging, lifelong confirmed skeptic
and a poet. You can almost automatically have my heart for two reasons:
make me laugh, or be an artist, any kind of artist. Jean was an artist—*and*
could make me laugh! And, as an alcoholic, she was also a consummate *artist*
at bull. But she was also the other kind of artist, a crafter of words.

Jean took whatever art was in my preaching and let it inspire her poetry. When she died of cancer at 72, she left behind a wonderful legacy of
poetry—except it was not organized.

The day I sold my car was a particularly difficult day for me. As I hur-
riedly emptied the glove box, a poem of Jean's fell out (she'd been dead
a year already). "How did this get in here?" I asked. Then I remembered:
when she stayed for the Sunday evening services or came on an occasional Wednesday night to church, I would sometimes drop her off on my
way home. Almost in lieu of carfare, she would often shove a poem
scrawled on an envelope or church bulletin into my hand.

The poem left in my glove box was one I had forgotten to "cash!"—left
unopened, uncashed for almost a year. There it was, lovely, fresh, and right
on time with what I needed. She was dead a whole year but still dazzling
me with her gifts.

Jean was a beloved if somewhat less than stellar graduate of the Alcoholism Center for Women, which is more a movement and community
than a "center." But in her last few years, Jean found a faith and relationship with God that matched the passion hidden in her religious skepti-
cism. She found her church in her community. It was just irreverent
enough, just real enough, and just open enough to art and irony so that
she could tolerate it.

When she was dying, I was in Mexico. But the day that she died, a lay
minister in our church, Woody, showed up at the hospital. Other people
from church began to arrive, and the nurses were irritated and skeptical:
"Who are these people?" Woody simply announced unequivocally that

they were all members of Jean's family. An African-American gay man, an Asian-American gay man, another white lesbian, and Woody. Family?! She died surrounded by those who would happily claim her as family. You *bet* they were her family. You couldn't have asked for a finer family, if a little unusual. Now, from time to time, gracefully, Jean's poems pop up in all sorts of odd places—in a pile of papers, in my car, in my heart and mind.

"Send Them"

The days prior to Christmas are always very busy in any church, and that is no less true for those of us at Metropolitan Community Church. Advent is often a frenzied time, as we try to add a dimension of piety, reflection, and *centeredness* to the cultural holiday bombardment. Since the industrial revolution in the West, and especially in the United States, Christian pastors seem doomed to fight this battle against commercialism, *putting Christ back into Christmas,* sometimes guilt-tripping our people as they try to walk their own tightropes of overspending, overeating, over-drinking, and other holiday compulsions.

Not only that, because the holidays are a time when Americans are most vulnerable to suicide, in overt or more subtle forms. Pastors get more late-night phone calls: there are more strangers calling for help than usual—for emotional, financial, or spiritual help. More folks end up in hospitals and emergency rooms. Funerals are twice as traumatic at holiday time.

This is even more true in minority communities. And it is much more stressful in the LGBT community. Alienation from family and traditional support structures (church of origin, for example) are felt much more deeply during holiday times. Some LGBT people are simply not "out" to their families, and they go home having to be extremely vague about their personal lives. This brings on feelings of guilt and shame and reinforces a sense of isolation. People feel compelled to lie about their relational life, friendships, and social, religious, or political activities. ("What did you say was the name of *that church* you're attending?") Some just avoid contact with their families. Or perhaps Mom and Dad know but ask you, beg you, *please* don't tell Grandma; it will kill her! Or don't come out to your fundamentalist brother-in-law. "Let's not argue at Christmas!"

Some people who come out to their families are told not to return home for the holidays—or at any time. Some couples, patiently trying to give their families space and time to "adjust," go their separate ways for the holidays, stealing a minute or two on an upstairs phone to wish their beloved "Merry Christmas," out of earshot for the family's sake.

Increasingly, there are couples or individuals who *finally* get to deal with just the usual family and in-law issues during the holiday season! What a red-letter day it is for a lesbian when she realizes that her mother has the same kinds of issues with her brothers' wives or sisters' husbands that she has with her partner! It is such an ironic sign of acceptance— when this lesbian can deal with ordinary family dynamics that are not primarily about homophobia! We need a family "graduation" ceremony at that point. Ordinary, garden-variety in-law conflicts are such a welcome relief!

For single LGBT folk, the holidays may be a time when they are pressured to date or marry heterosexually—another good reason to come out!

Holiday times are a special challenge in our church. In addition to the usual Advent services and midmonth church and staff Christmas parties, we hold workshops designed to help people "beat the holiday blues." We go Christmas caroling at gay bars and in hospices, and we try to provide alternative family events, helping people deal with their present status vis-a-vis their families and providing extra support. Some people leave for home for the holidays and let us know they plan to come out to their families. Sometimes, that's out of a strength of conviction or a need to be honest. Sometimes, it occurs in the midst of coming out about HIV or AIDS. In any case, we send people off with promises of prayer, support, and hugs.

At MCC Los Angeles, we also always offered a Christmas Day Open House. We realized that many times people from MCC would go home after a Christmas Eve service to a long, lonely Christmas Day. Some people need an excuse to leave uncomfortable family scenes ("I'm needed at my church today, Mom!") or a place to hang out, with food and friendly faces.

Ben Rodermond loved food. At special church occasions, he would always bring a treat, something sweet and fattening. His blue eyes twinkled with mischief, his ruddy complexion partially hidden by a Vandyke beard and a waxed, old-fashioned, handlebar mustache. Soft-spoken and a little shy, he retained his distinct Dutch accent. Ben was a large, tall man who rode a motorcycle, but you instantly sensed he was a gentle, kind person.

Ben loved all kinds of good food, including Indonesian food. He went to Indonesia after World War II. Then he came to the United States, where gradually in the Fifties and Sixties he began to find other gay people. Ben was there in the earliest days of MCC, feeling a strong, passionate connection to the social Gospel preached by Troy Perry. Even though Ben was not a citizen at the time and was risking more than most people, he stood openly with Troy at the first demonstrations for gay rights in Los Angeles.

Ben also loved food because he knew what it was to be hungry. Ben and his sister Henny and other members of their family had hidden Jews in their home in Holland during the Nazi occupation.

To avoid being conscripted into the Nazi army, Ben went underground for many years as a teenager. Part of the time, he hid in a small attic crawl space while his sister brought him what little food they had, along with news from the BBC. Part of the time, he roamed the streets and nearly starved to death there. But he survived. Eventually, Ben found friends, LGBT brothers and sisters, and a spiritual home at Metropolitan Community Church of Los Angeles. He had no patience for injustice, for bigotry of any kind. And he had a permanent sweet tooth.

Back to my story. I try to schedule very little during Christmas week, just to leave room for the unexpected and to be able (while choirs are rehearsing, deacons are decorating the church, and logistical problems are being resolved!) to be free to reach out beyond our church walls a little to those who are more marginalized, especially in this season. So that was how I happened to meet Michael on Christmas Eve, 1992.

We had three Christmas Eve services scheduled for that evening, two in English and one in Spanish. The bulletins were done. The church on Washington Boulevard was filled with evergreens. We prayed that it would not be too cold (as it can get in the L.A. desert climate), as our inadequate heater seemed only to *taunt* us with the hope that it might actually heat up the sanctuary.

My sermons were also done: one for the earlier crowd that included more seniors and people with young children, and one for the more lively "midnight mass" group, on their way to or from Christmas parties or family gatherings. This was one of the occasions in the year when people brought straight parents, children, and family members or LGBT friends who wouldn't be caught dead in church on an ordinary Sunday but for whom it was *cool* to show up on Christmas Eve.

So I had the entire day *free* on Christmas Eve, which is what I had planned. There were no last-minute emergencies and only one person in the hospital (which would be my last stop before getting to the church office later that evening).

I decided to stop by three hospices on my way into town. I have always been told by hospice and hospital staff that churches and groups visit patients (especially those without families) all during the weeks up to Christmas but that the visits come to a halt on Christmas Eve and Christmas Day. Most people, including clergy, are simply too busy on those days with their own families and church business. So it felt like my unplanned Christmas Eve and Day visits were more needed and possibly more timely. I set out to visit with a kind of quiet hopefulness, not knowing what would await me.

The first place I went was a hospice I had visited a great many times. At least half a dozen of our members had died of AIDS in this hospice. I knew many people on the staff, some of whom were members of MCC or who had associations with us over the years. So they didn't look too surprised to see me.

It was a foggy day. The hospice was nestled in a wooded area near a park in downtown L.A. It is a small facility, with a comfortable living room and a devoted staff. This Christmas Eve, it was quiet in a kind of eerie way. When I arrived, everything seemed so still. All the holiday hubbub was over before it had begun. There were no family members hanging around, as there often are. No music was playing.

I asked the staff if there was anyone who needed a visit from me today. Two staff members looked at each other and communicated nonverbally. Then the nursing coordinator, a man, said, "Well, there's Michael—he's having a hard time." They related to me that they had had a Christmas party the day before. Michael was too upset and maybe too angry and ill to come out of his room. They said that Michael was physically very near death, ready to die, but he seemed anxious and afraid. They knew nothing about his religious issues. But they said, "He just can't let go." They told me he was 25 years old and had a sister. With that little bit of information, I knocked on Michael's door and entered. Even with all the death and dying I had seen, I wasn't quite prepared for this one.

Michael was young. Though probably of average height, he weighed only about 75 pounds. For some reason (unusual in a hospice), he had a nasal-gastric tube and tubes coming out of his mouth and abdomen. He looked a little alarmed when I entered the room. I sat down, telling him I was a minister. (I thought my clerical collar might have alarmed him, as in "A clergyperson I don't recognize has come to see me—the end must be near!")

He had a notebook by his head, and he lay facing me on his left side. With his right hand, he held a pencil, and I noticed a lot of scrawls on the notebook. Michael was communicating by means of this notebook, because he could not talk with the tubes in his nose and throat. His face was filled with pain and fear. He struggled to position himself so he could write on the notebook. It took quite some time for that to happen. I also realized that he was so weak that he could barely press hard enough to make a recognizable mark on the pad.

I panicked. What the hell was I doing here? I thought to myself, How are we going to communicate? Maybe I'm just frightening him *more*. I felt guilty for feeling uncomfortable. I wanted to flee from the room. I knew that only Michael, God, and I would know the truth if I just left. Whose big idea was it to come here on Christmas Eve, anyway? No normal person would have chosen to be here! Was I trying to be heroic? Brave? A glutton for punishment? And now I was making this kid's suffering worse!

As I thought these thoughts, Michael had finally gotten pencil in hand. "Help," he wrote. That took two minutes to write. *Help.* "Killing me," he wrote. Then he pulled on his gastric tube, writhing in pain. Perhaps he thinks the members of the staff here are trying to kill him. Does he have dementia? Or is he just angry, exhausted, and a little disoriented with his weakness and the medication? There was no way to know for certain.

So I spoke: "Michael, I know you are in terrible pain. No one is trying to kill you, Michael." I touched his head with my hand. "You are dying, and they are trying to help you have less pain and discomfort."

At that point, a tear came down his cheek. Michael struggled again to write, with agonizing slowness. He wrote again, "Help me."

I wanted to run. I have never wanted to leave a room so much in my life. Obviously, I wasn't getting through, and I was frustrating him. But I touched his head again and said, "Michael, I don't know if I can help you or not. All I can do is pray for you. Do you want me to?" He seemed to nod, but I wasn't sure. So I gambled and went for it. I placed both my hands on him and prayed about his fear. I prayed that he could trust God a little more. I prayed for the pain to decrease and cease, for him to be able to relax and trust God, who loved him. As I prayed, I could feel his tears on my hands. Then I felt my own tears.

We opened our eyes. He wanted to write again. This time, the writing came swiftly, mercifully. In a flourish he wrote, "This is a hospice. Christmas Eve. What are you doing here?"

Great question! I had asked it myself about 20 minutes earlier. I laughed a little and said, "Well, right now, Michael, I'm crying with you." Then I noticed the Bible underneath his notebook.

"What church?" he wrote.

"Metropolitan Community Church." He showed no sign of recognition. Imagine that—someone in Los Angeles who had never heard of MCC! So, as succinctly as I could, I told him *the* story. I had to assume at this point that it was likely that Michael *was* gay. I told him I was gay and about Troy Perry and MCC. I could see he had never heard of our ministry or about the fact that one could be gay and Christian. His eyes brimmed with tears; he even seemed to smile just a little, in between what looked like *electrical* jolts of pain. I talked a mile a minute, flooding the room with every reassurance I could manage to speak with confidence.

When I took a breath, he wrote, "Angels?" I said yes, I believed in angels and that he had the name of the greatest angel, the archangel Michael. Then he wrote, "Gay angels?"

"Gay angels?" It all came clear. Michael did not want to go anywhere he would not be welcome, including heaven (maybe especially). But, if gay angels would accompany him, there was hope!

Suddenly, I remembered Ben Rodermond from Holland, who had died only three months before in the room next door to Michael's. Ben was an angel, in life and in death. I could see Ben's face suddenly; I could see him coming for Michael, bringing his little gay brother to the throne of grace, holding his hand, healing his fear. "Yes, Michael, there are gay angels: one of them died a few months ago in the next room," I said. Gay angels, what a wonderful thought; the room seemed to be filled with them. "Thank you, God," I kept saying in my heart.

Then Michael wrote again: "Send them."

He was ready now, and somehow he thought I had the ability, the authority to send the gay angels for him. So I prayed again for that very thing.

Michael seemed calmer. His eyelids rested a little. Gently, I touched his face and hands and kissed him good-bye.

That night at the Christmas Eve service, in our very cold sanctuary, we prayed for Michael. I called the hospice the next morning; Michael had died in the wee hours of that Christmas morning, led to his Maker, I'm sure, by Ben and his fellow gay angels.

5 • A Queer Theology of Sexuality

If we were really about to propose a "queer millennium," part of what might characterize this new era would be a new theology of sexuality.

Many of us in the LGBT religious community have talked about this for a long time. We have struggled to understand how feminist critique and gay and lesbian experience might not just *add to* a theology of sexuality but might be able to reframe the discussion. This has been difficult because, for the most part, we have seen our theological agenda as trying to "normalize" gay sexuality for the public, struggling for our human rights, wanting simply to be included in the panorama of human life. We've been bogged down by the necessity to do biblical or theological *apologetics*. But what if we actually claimed a role in *reshaping the basic questions* concerning God and human sexuality?

Every time mainline denominations in the United States try to "study" the issue of homosexuality, the study group always realizes that it cannot study homosexuality in isolation. The issue of human sexuality is the locus of most of our real, deep conflicts, and this is the reason we cannot seem to talk about homosexuality rationally or with a sense of ease or comfort.

A National Council of Churches of Christ staff member noticed that, when she was assigned to one of the three or four dialogue committees on MCC or on homosexuality that were commissioned by the NCC over a ten-year period, she suddenly found herself becoming the de facto "sex expert and counselor" at the office. Everyone began consciously or unconsciously to assume that she had skills or expertise (or a sense of openness and compassion) that she was not sure she could honestly claim for herself. She said, "When conversations at the water fountain became incredibly interesting, complicated, and intimate, the single contributing factor to their changed perception of me was my staff connection to our study group!"

This is where the stories of Sodom and Gomorrah and Gibeah become very useful again. If the sin of Sodom is *not* gay or lesbian sexuality—if it really is about violence and particularly sexualized violence—then we have a new place to begin. The sins of Sodom and Gibeah were about the violent uses of sexuality, the punishment of the "other," those who are different for reasons of race, gender, sexuality, or culture (or religion, perhaps). It is the hatred of the other, acted out in violence and sexual abuse. It is certainly much too euphemistic to call this behavior *inhospitality*.

However, we can turn this around and ask the question: What is the nature of godly, healthy sexual contact, and is it possible to use the concept of hospitality as a positive model for theological reflection about sexuality? Could the concept of *bodily hospitality* be useful in beginning to construct a new theology of sexuality and sexual relating that is somewhat free from old sexual rules and roles? Could it be a first step that would inform and undergird a new and healthier sexual ethic?

Sexual Hospitality as a "Queer" Gift

Hospitality, as I have stated earlier, is a spiritual gift that has decidedly "queer" connections. There are profound differences among LGBT people in this regard, but I think this idea works for all of our communities. One stereotype of gay men is that they are *fabulous* cooks and hosts of great parties. Perhaps this connection of hospitality and gays is as simple as the notion of a "queer sensibility": the love of gay men for elegance, for hospitality as an *art form*. Certainly, there are gay men who are slobs or who can't cook or decorate or set a gorgeous table, but it does seem like there are a disproportionate number of them who do have a *flair* for hospitality of this kind. This has cultural and historical roots, which Judy Grahn has traced, calling us "trans-people," people of the world between genders. Our job is partly to be cultural go-betweens. Eunuchs of old, we recall, were "court officials"; many were gay and responsible for *palace hospitality*.

In England recently, I spoke with a gay man who had been the butler to a high-ranking member of Parliament. He told me that the royal family preferred gay men as palace servants because they were the *best* at providing hospitality of all kinds. Why has this queer stereotype persisted for thousands of years? Saying all this always means walking a narrow tightrope:

speaking of gayness in essentialist terms can simply reinforce stereotypes. Even *neutral* or *positive* stereotypes can be used in politically dangerous ways. When I think of lesbians and lesbian culture, I think of potlucks and an easy flow of work, preparation, food and home, sex, and friends. For lesbians, hospitality is hardly ever *formal.* It is fluid, communal, and easy, with everyone pitching in and not a lot of ownership of the "product." Also, it may be characterized by permeable boundaries that include parents and children and other family members, as well as bisexuals and men.

Perhaps the experience of having been left out or put out of our homes and families (even if we later reconcile with them and heal the rift) makes us more willing and open to inviting and accepting each other into our homes—our living rooms, kitchens, and, sometimes, bedrooms.

I have a collection of particular holiday memories from the first few years after Paula and I arrived in California. In the early Eighties, during the second year we were here, we rented a fairly large house, which we could afford because we had a roommate at the time. It was Thanksgiving, in the year of the U.S. Cuban refugee resettlement. MCC churches got involved with resettling hundreds of LGBT Cuban refugees. One of Paula's former students was stationed nearby in the marines and was too far from home to go back for the holiday. We invited ten or so friends, the student, my cousin Linton, the MCC pastor who was the chaplain for the refugees, about five refugees, and some others whom I've forgotten. Most of these folks were gay or lesbian, but not all. Every day of the week before, Paula and I would find out that we had each separately invited someone else. I think there were 35 or so people there. We actually managed to seat everyone in two rooms and at tables outside (this was Thanksgiving in California). I cooked the turkeys and basic vegetables; others brought their own dishes. The Cubans (mostly drag queens and one lesbian) experienced their first traditional (hah!) U.S. Thanksgiving, which included stuffed artichokes, Mexican lasagna, a California fruit salad, a few Asian dishes, turkey, and dressing.

Other years, we'd have family members of the people I had pastored who had died of AIDS. For most holidays over the last eight or ten years, someone with AIDS or HIV or who was recently bereaved (that's most of us) has been at our table. It's just a fact of life.

Each holiday has produced its own one-time-only extended family du jour. This is not a *hobby.* It is a way of living and being. It is an adventure, and it has a lot to do with being lesbian. It has everything to do with how we view life and relationships, with our own emerging values. It has to do with our own (for better or worse) family histories, how we both react in opposition to them, and how we sometimes unconsciously recreate them. It has to do with a belief that our home, our time, our table, our resources, our skills, our affection, and our capacity to live are to be *shared*. The sharing should support, nourish, and enrich others and ourselves, maybe for a day or maybe for years.

Many LGBT people consciously create environments of hospitality in their homes or organizations. They do this as a gift, a way of life. And I don't mean to suggest that straight people don't do this. But there is something, perhaps, about being "unhinged" from the conventional family constructs that opens up the opportunities, the desire both to deconstruct and to reconstruct this aspect of our lives. In fact, these days, as straight people have to deal with in-laws from more than one marriage, or divorced parents have to develop a holiday "schedule" with their kids—in other words, as predominantly heterosexual families get more complicated—they begin to resemble LGBT families more and more!

Bodily Hospitality

The Bible itself speaks of the human body as the "temple" of the spirit. Our bodies are our *home*. Our body/self is the home, the locus, of our identity.

In *People of the Deer*, Farley Mowatt describes his own learning experience with Native Canadians who hunt the vanishing caribou. He lived with them for a time and at first felt very critical of the shelters that they built.[26] These were nomadic people. To Mowatt, their shelters seemed flimsy and inadequate. He could think of many ways to improve them! Gradually, it dawned on him that the shelters were built this way because they were not these people's actual *homes*. The shelters only served to cut down on the extreme winds and the snow or rain, but the Native Canadians' true *shelters* or homes were their own *bodies*, covered by the skins of the caribou. Their clothing was carefully made and was all the shelter they needed. Their bodies had been honed, toughened, and adapted to their primary need for warmth and protection. They carried their homes with them on and *in* their own bodies in a way that made our view of home (as a building) superfluous.

Some of us, particularly nonnative people, have difficulty identifying with our bodies or understanding our bodies as our homes. We are terribly disconnected from our bodies, as if our bodies are a *thing* to be dealt with—as if we are *not* our bodies or at least not *in* our bodies.[27]

Dwelling in Our Bodies/Homes

But our bodies are *home. I* think of that when I think of the purpose and importance of our skin, for instance. Our skin serves a number of simultaneous functions: it is the first element in our body's immune system—keeping out germs, disease, and infection. It is simultaneously the *organ* through which we experience one of our five senses—the sense of touch. Our skin is also an important participant in our sexual response system. It is the means through which we touch and experience the touch of others. We are constantly having to interpret with our minds and hearts the meaning of the ways in which we are touching and being touched. Our skin is the locus of erogenous zones that are mysteriously and powerfully connected to our sexuality. Our skin is also the primary identifying characteristic of race. Along with the marks of our gender, it becomes the most highly politicized component of our body.

Our skin, therefore, symbolizes and embodies both our *immunity* and our *vulnerability* (physically *and* politically).

I have seen this poignantly illustrated in the experience of people with AIDS. When persons with AIDS experience an opening in their skin through a cut or sore, they do not heal as well because their immune system is not functioning properly. At the same time, the skin itself is a part of the immune system. So the effect is compounded. As the skin breaks down, it acts very much like a home whose roof or walls or floors have holes. The rupturing of this protective layer creates a new kind of vulnerability. Many persons with AIDS, like burn victims, have lost the outer layer of their defense system against disease because of severe skin disease. Suddenly, the skin, rather than being an organ of safety or defense, is itself the *enemy.* It becomes the cause of suffering, pain, intrusion, even death.

People with AIDS respond in various ways to this experience. For some, it opens them up and helps them become more emotionally vulnerable. For others, it necessitates doubling their emotional defenses.

My friend Rick was a handsome, effeminate gay man who loved to clown around. He was an artist and had gorgeous, prematurely gray hair (he was in his early thirties), full lips, and bright blue eyes. When Rick got AIDS, he was infected with something called psoriatic arthritis, a painful and disfiguring joint disease that also erupted in psoriasis all over his body. When I hadn't seen him at work in a few weeks (he worked across the hall from an office I frequented), I called him at home; I knew he must be very sick.

When I went to see him, his feet were triple their normal size and almost black. He had psoriasis on nearly 75 percent of his body. He could barely hobble to the bathroom and hadn't eaten in days. The psoriasis was in his hair and eyebrows, in what was left of his full beard and mustache, inside his mouth, under his eyelids, and inside his ears. In his bed and on the floor were layers of his skin that he had shed. I could have filled a wastebasket with the shed skin. He cried, and I cried. I told him he had to go to the hospital. He didn't want to go. I told him if he didn't go voluntarily, I would have to call an ambulance (I wasn't even sure they would take him). I told him if he didn't go, he was going to lose his feet, although I didn't really think they could save them at this point. Finally, he agreed to go. I talked three members of our AIDS ministry team into taking him to the hospital. They carried him down the stairs while he alternately joked and cried. They had to leave all the windows in the car open because the stench was so bad. He was literally rotting from the outside in.

Rick lived almost another six months. They never had to amputate his feet, but neither his feet nor the psoriasis got much better. In the last weeks of his life, he could not be touched almost at all because of the excruciating pain and because of the danger to others of the gangrenous infection that covered so much of his body. Yet, just before Christmas, Rick was still able to joke and laugh and relate. I will never know how.

The last time I went to see him, they would not let me in the room, though his mother was able to be with him off and on. The doctors were with him at the time, and it was just too stressful for him to see anyone else. I sat out in the hospice dining room and kept hearing this high-pitched scream. It was weeks before I could really allow myself to know that *that sound* had come from Rick. He was so exhausted, his strength so depleted, that he could only cry out in a high-pitched wail that sounded like a child. Now and then, unfortunately, I can still recall it.

He died on New Year's Eve, not wanting, I'm sure, to enter another year with such unrelenting pain and suffering.

I remember that, for weeks after that, I would look at and touch my own skin and think of how the smallest cut or blemish can annoy or embarrass me. I wondered at the health of my own skin, at how, even with my aging process, it is still relatively smooth and healthy and resilient, and at how I take my own skin for granted. I wondered at the mystery of skin in different places on my own body—the calloused parts, the tender parts— and how it loosens with age. I considered how the *accidents* of gender, race, genetics, and disease bring such incredible power and meaning to the color and texture of our skin. I wonder still at the politics of my skin, which is the living "wall" of my body/home. How does the outer relate to the inner? To the colors and texture of our *walls* and *floors* and *roof*?

An acupuncturist friend of mine told me that in Chinese medicine and philosophy the skin is primarily related to the lungs and to breathing. This is why, she said, people with respiratory problems also often have skin problems. Recent diagnostic descriptions of asthma, for instance, include skin problems as a symptom of the disease. Our lungs, necessary for breathing, for life itself, can also be the pathway of infection and disease, a way in which we can take in toxins, allergens, and germs.

Sexuality, too, especially in the age of AIDS, contains this paradox. Sexuality can be the means of tremendous self-expression, power, desire, and fulfillment of the urge to connect with others. It can also be the way in which we experience shame and abuse, disappointment, isolation, obsession, and violence.

This is the physical, graphic way in which we know the paradox of living: to live is to risk, often even to risk life itself! Jesus said paradoxical stuff like this all the time: to save your life, lose it! By dying, we Christians believe, Christ gave us the gift of eternal life. Jesus (I once heard someone say in a very oversimplified explanation of the incarnation) is God with *skin* on—God risking God's self in human flesh and vulnerability.

The Jesus who said he wanted to be identified with "the least of these" today has AIDS, including Kaposi's sarcoma and life-threatening psoriasis in the skin that *contains* divinity.

Bodily Differences: The Politics of Ownership

It is interesting to compare the differences in our bodies with the differences in our homes. Some of us own our own homes. We have a sense that we can control them—decorate, remodel, improve, neglect, or furnish our homes in any way we please. Similarly, some of us have a consciousness about our bodies, an intentionality. We believe we can or should control our weight, hairstyle, shape, and so on.

Others of us do not believe that our bodies are our own. Many children, maybe even most children, have a sense that they are not ultimately in control of their own bodies. Parents, or guardians, or sometimes even older children or other adults may seem to "possess" a child or his or her body. Sometimes, this is done out of seemingly good motives—to protect, for instance. In other cases, it may be in order to exploit the child. Many children have to *struggle* for privacy, for a sense of boundaries, and for even a clear idea that their own body is really their own body and not the "property" of someone else.

Many parents believe that, in a sense, they own their children, just as they think they own the bodies of their pets or plants (also a primarily-Western modern idea). This goes on long after the natural developmental process of separation and individuation has occurred or *should* have occurred. Many women feel as if their fathers or husbands own their bodies, as if they cannot make independent choices about their own bodies. For some, this lack of ownership is less obvious. It is framed simply as a desire to *please* another—a spouse or partner. This desire is reflected in the belief that one should shape or decorate or clothe one's body in a way that pleases the other, without thinking about what pleases *oneself*. Men also do this, although to a lesser extent.

People sometimes "lease" their bodies, renting them out. There are women who lease their bodies for the purpose of procreation, as in surrogate parenting. There are others who less formally lease or rent out their bodies but do so nevertheless—who exchange their bodies for shelter, food, clothing, warmth, affection, addictions, or money.

If you are in prison, you soon learn that you do not own your own body. "They" get to control a lot of things about your body: what you eat, what you wear, when and where you sleep, your health, and where you spend your time. They can control your contact with those to whom you speak, touch, and communicate. There is no right to privacy, no matter what they promise.

This happens to people in other institutions, even to those who are supposedly *not* being punished. Certainly, it happens to people in hospitals, nursing homes, and shelters.

The reality of the politics of how much control we have over our own bodies and under what circumstances is staggering. Some of us *say* we own our home—but the truth is, the bank or mortgage company really owns it! We're *working* toward owning it. We may actually get to own it before we die, if we don't sell it or remortgage it! Very few people who say they own their homes actually own them "free and clear."

Free and clear: What a concept! I remember how I felt in high school when I knew I wanted to get out of the suburban town I lived in and never come back. I knew the way to do this was to go to college, for which I had no money. Going away to college seemed to be the method of getting free and clear. I knew I couldn't bear to stay home and go to a local college. I didn't even really know why—I just wanted out. Something about growing up in the era I did, where I did, I never quite felt like my body, or time, or life was really my own. I always felt like I owed somebody something. I'm sure my parents also felt that way growing up. It wasn't that I lacked what I needed or didn't feel loved. It was something other than that, a system of assumptions in which I lived. So I went to work in an electronics factory and began to save up to go to college. My mother also got a job in anticipation of having three children who would probably all move away and go to college.

All through high school and during summers and vacations from college, I worked in that factory. I hated it. The pay was lousy, but I could work overtime. The only thing that kept me from going crazy was the knowledge that I was doing this so that I would never have to do this again. I was literally selling my hours, my time, and my body/self so that I could leave, so that I could have more choices about how to spend my time. I remember feeling angry that, because I was a young female with few marketable skills that suited the opportunities available in that industrial park, my time and my body/self were worth so little. I felt the grief of lost hours, days, even years, sold to make fuel boxes for airplanes so I could get out of there.

As children, adolescents, then young adults, we struggle to have a sense of identity and independence vis-a-vis our body/selves—physically, mentally, emotionally, even spiritually. What does it mean for us really to have a sense of control over our own bodies? Women have special issues about this related to the fact that we can potentially "share" our bodies in the process of conception and birth. The whole abortion debate is centered around a woman's right to determine whether or not her body will or will not be used to house the embryonic life of another human being. Being pregnant is a very powerful and unique experience of *bodily hospitality*. What does it mean to share the inside of your body, your food and blood and energy and every single minute of every single day for about nine months with someone you don't even know yet? How does this change your view of your own body, the whole concept of hospitality?

How does our sense of being at home or not being at home in our own bodies affect how well we are able to share our bodies when we want or need to do so?

I think of women who are addicted to drugs or alcohol or who smoke, and get pregnant. How does it feel to them no longer to have the freedom to risk abusing their bodies in certain ways, because another person's life and health are at stake and have intruded in their lives? And, if many of those with such addictions have problems with self-esteem and loving their own body/self, how can they possibly love this unknown other more than they love themselves? Some women with little support, resources, money, family, friends, or hope are *tremendously* courageous as they attempt to take care of their bodies in new ways—unfortunately, *not* because they love themselves but because they are trying to be a better "host" to a new life.

It also takes courage for some women to face the fact that they are not equipped to share their body with another at a particular time—that saying an honest "no" now may mean a more healthy and wise "yes" later.

In the early days of gay and lesbian liberation, I came out in the city of Boston. In 1972, there was only one lesbian bar in Boston, and it was located in the "combat zone," an area of several blocks in downtown Boston that used to house porno theaters, nightclubs, strip joints, leather bars, and gay bars. My friend Julie says it was called the combat zone because MPs patrolled the area during World War II to protect GIs on weekend passes.

There was a constant turf war among the city, police, various Mafia interests, and "legitimate" business interests. But the weapons of the war were sex and drugs. And the *victims* were the patrons and providers, the sexual outlaws, the young and restless, the old and frustrated, the lost and lonely, the adventurous.

Jacques's was a notorious place that had a heterosexual prostitute bar in front, with a "lesbian room" with a pool table in the back, and a leather bar in the basement. I was 22, just out of the closet, and had only been to one other gay bar in my life. (I'd been to Forty-Second Street in New York, but only in the daytime!) I was in seminary at the time and had just barely found MCC. I was curious about this lesbian bar. So I went there, twice.

I remember trying not to dress too much like a tourist or college student. I felt shy and totally out of place walking by the older women sex workers perched on bar stools in the front corridor. I remember wanting to look at them and wanting to avoid looking at them all at the same time. Both times, I was too afraid to descend to the leather bar downstairs. I didn't really understand what that "scene" was about. The first time, my experience in the lesbian "area" at Jacques's was okay, no big deal. Tough-looking middle-aged lesbians competed good-naturedly at the pool table. I nursed a beer for about an hour and went home grateful to have gone unnoticed.

The next time I went, about half an hour into my sojourn, beer bottles started flying across the room, and the next thing I knew we could hear sirens and police entering the front door, where the women sex workers perched. There was a mad dash for the back door as women vaulted over the pool table and knocked over furniture to get out. As we were trying to leave, we literally ran into guys in leather, as well as some drag queens, who were rushing up and out of the basement. Jacques's was closed down soon after.

Years later, I would sit with the older lesbians at the new lesbian-owned, non-Mafia bar called the Saints. These older dykes loved to entertain us with stories about the "good old days" at Jacques's and other combat-zone clubs. They wore their scars like badges of courage! They told how the cops came to know them by name after a while, sometimes letting them crawl voluntarily into the paddy wagons without the customary beatings on backs, legs, and heads. Sometimes, they were so drunk and disorderly they reasoned that they kind of *deserved* the treatment they got. They loved to play "top this," sharing tall tales about their experiences of danger and violence, how they *got away* with flipping the finger at life, the cops, and God. Defiantly queer, they recounted rituals of cross-dressing, drinking, posturing, raids, cops, and jail—all lived within the parameters of having to go to work or being in the closet to some degree. Secrets, danger, defiance, shame, and submission—all were the elements of queer life, pre-Stonewall.

Twenty years later, I would meet a heterosexual woman who knew some women *I* had known at combat-zone strip joints in Boston, clubs like the Two o'Clock Club and the Mouse Trap. Most of these bars were owned by organized crime organizations. All sorts of illegal activities went on there (including drugs, gambling, and prostitution). They paid off the police not to shut them down. The police had to raid these clubs every once in a while just to make it look good to the citizenry. The gay bars were the easiest to raid because the queers wouldn't object. They were used to it; they expected it. No one would stand up for them.

Julie grew up in the suburbs of Boston, in what she describes as a "nice Jewish home." But she struggled very hard to have a sense of herself, her body/self. At about age 19, after a brief failed marriage that included a stint of rural "living on the land," Julie came home to her parents' house. One day, she started dancing in the living room when they were not at home. She described this experience of loving to dance as an experience of loving her own body, of enjoying looking at herself in the mirror as she danced. She got this idea in her head that she could be a go-go dancer in one of "those clubs" she had heard about in downtown Boston (like the 1970s TV show *Hullabaloo,* she thought).

Julie was very naive. She did not know what these clubs were really about. But she found them, found out, and decided to become a dancer there anyway. She was young (most of the strippers in these clubs were well into their lifelong careers!) and a great dancer with a beautiful body. Julie learned quickly and well and loved to perform, to be watched, to dance. Somehow she managed to escape hard-core drug addiction, although she used drugs (setting a boundary at not shooting up). She participated in extensive sexual experimentation, but she never yielded to the pressure to participate in the prostitution business that boomed in these clubs. Julie was already amazed by the money she made stripping, but she could have more than tripled that amount by just turning a few tricks.

She told me her story with a mix of enjoyment and sadness, sharing this secret of her past and how exotic and adventurous it seemed. She hinted at all the pain and the stresses and confusion inherent in such a life. For instance, two weeks after starting her dancing career, her parents found out and threw her out of the house. They called her names worse than those she heard in the clubs. Her brother came after her with a knife.

In some strange way, there was some healing for Julie in telling *me* her story. I'd been to some of those clubs and others just like them. I'd been there as a clergyperson trying to find "my people" and as a patron shyly trying to discover something about myself and my own sexuality. Like Julie, I'd grown up very sheltered about sexuality and my options, with no sense of being at home in my own body.

I also had to chuckle because I vaguely recognized Julie's description of how she felt looking in the mirror and being a performer. As a person who gets up in front of crowds a few times a week, I, too, am a performer. Preaching is, or can be, performance art, especially in this television age. I have to use my whole body/self when I preach. In order to keep people's attention (people who are used to looking at television or lots of action), I have to work at it. Part of my preaching task is to help people who are often numbed by oppression or by the competing messages and pressures of the world to *feel*. I have to help them feel so that they can also think about and find a relationship to their own spirituality and a relationship to God.

And there is something interesting about comparing preaching as a performance art to stripping! Sometimes I do have to strip down. I have to be real. I have to share not just my thoughts but my heart, my fears, and my struggles. Sometimes I have to *bare my soul*. My preacher friend Judy Dahl describes one experience of getting up to preach on Sunday at her church and just confessing, "I have no business being up here today, but we preachers often preach what we need to hear ourselves."

What Julie and other women who worked in those places did was to provide several "services." The strip shows were entertainment, but they were much more. Sometimes, they were the only sexual stimulation and experience some people had. For others, they were a form of sex education. They occurred in a sleazy environment, but they were still education—education that was *not* happening, by the way, in the wider society of this sexually repressed and obsessed culture.

Also, these places were offering a kind of hospitality. They offered hospitality to the fantasies and the repressed longings for sexual contact—or for contact of any kind, perhaps. Lonely, desperate people who felt unfulfilled and suppressed, or that somehow their own sexual needs and desires were unacceptable anywhere else, felt welcomed and, to some degree, acceptable in these places. Women like Julie—young, beautiful, enjoying their own bodies, and putting on a show—invited those who watched to feel and to fantasize. In the combat zone, those "anything goes" zones, there was ironically a profound sense of safety and permission, partly made possible by anonymity. There were also sometimes profound shame and guilt. There were danger and crime. There was risk of arrest or punishment (unless you were really rich and famous and could buy everyone off). So this hospitality was very costly. It was costly also to many of those women, who, having entered this "glamorous" life, often never got off the merry-go-round of drugs and prostitution. Many of them died of overdoses or of being beaten to death by pimps, boyfriends, or tricks.

When Julie and I talked, she really warmed to the story. Because I'd been there, too, she didn't feel *judged*. We knew some of the same people. We were struggling to understand our early adulthood experiences of trying to feel at home in our own bodies and what it meant to share our body/selves with those who needed *hospitality*.

The first stripper I ever met, I met at church. Her stage name was "Frosty Winters." She was a headliner at the Two o'Clock Club. Her name came from her act. Apparently, in a certain lighting, her skin had a somewhat green-gray-mint tinge. She built her act around this physical "special effect." And she was a lesbian. Lots of these women were bisexuals or lesbians. (Julie was shocked when I told her this.) Women who stripped for men, for money, some of whom also turned tricks for money, were also sometimes lesbians. They had a private life on *the side,* usually with a butch who often resented like hell that her "fem" stripped for men or turned tricks.

Frosty and her partner, Claire, found MCC Boston in the first few weeks of our existence there in 1972. They had first heard of MCC while living in Florida (a lot of strippers worked Florida clubs in the winter). Claire, though butch by most standards, had also been heterosexually married, had five older kids (none of whom were with her), and a brand-new baby boy. Claire contacted the church because she wanted Eric to be baptized. She was the first lesbian mother I ever met.

I visited Frosty and Claire in their little apartment in the South End of Boston. I have to admit, I was fascinated by Frosty and her career, and this was probably the reason I checked out the combat zone in the first place. I was also doing "missionary work," dropping off church ads and cards in the clubs and in the gay section of the porno shops. (There were no gay newspapers or organizations or coffeehouses to take them to!)

Frosty and Claire were warm and hospitable to me. I never told anyone how old I was in those days because I thought I was probably too young to be pastoring. I worried about my credibility. I suspect they knew anyway, but they were sweet to me and treated me just like I was an adult and a *real* pastor!

Eric was my first infant baptism. He was an adorable six-month-old, a blond, healthy baby. It thrilled me to touch him with the water, to hold him in my arms, and to welcome him to the people of God who called themselves MCC Boston, meeting at the Arlington Street Unitarian Church.

Two weeks later, I got a late-night call from Claire. She was hysterical. She sounded drunk. Frosty was *moving out,* leaving her. Could I come over now? I put on my clerical collar and took the bus to the South End, enduring the stares of all who had never seen a woman in a collar. (Well, a collar *and* a blue jean jacket.) When I got there, it was quite a scene. Frosty, as it turned out, had an expensive heroin habit, and Claire was tired of it. Frosty didn't want to be lectured or controlled. Claire was worried about Frosty's dealer and the danger to themselves and the baby. Frosty, wearing dark glasses, and looking like hell, was leaving with her bags; she gave me a "Sorry, kid" look as she exited.

Claire was crying (as was the baby), and I finally noticed the gun. Claire was threatening to kill herself with it, and she raced out of the house. I followed her. I grabbed her and spun her around, and she pointed the gun at my stomach and said, "If you try to stop me, I'll blow you away."

Now, I had never seen a real handgun. I'd seen my Grandpa's rifles, mostly sitting high up on a rack at the farm. But I'd never seen anything but a toy handgun.

This was one of those "pastoral moments" that neither the Religion Department at Allegheny College nor my six weeks of seminary had prepared me for. There was no time for "theological reflection" (unless you count the prayer that went something like "Oh, crap!"). There was no time really to consider the options. I think I did believe that, if I let her go, she would shoot herself. For some strange reason (maybe because I knew she'd been a Catholic), I didn't believe she would really shoot me. Of course, this could simply have been denial! There was no time to sort that out, however. I mustered up all the "priestly authority" I could manage and said sternly and, I hoped, convincingly, "Give me that gun!"

She did. She just handed me the gun. Now, I'd never *held* a real gun either, and when its heaviness landed in the palm of my hand, so did the realization of what had just happened or nearly happened. My knees got wobbly. Claire must have sensed this, and she proceeded to help me into the house. She was also starting to enter the weepy phase of her drunkenness. So we sat in the apartment, the gun underneath my jacket next to me on the couch, as I held Claire while she cried. And the baby was crying, too.

There was no manual for this. I left my home address and phone number on the kitchen table, covered the sleeping Claire with a blanket, took the gun, Eric, a few diapers, and a bottle, and caught the bus home.

Claire got sober for a while, but eventually drank again and lost Eric to the foster care system. Years later, Claire caught up with me, when she got sober again, and she told me that Eric had graduated from high school and was in touch with her again.

A lot of my ministry and the ministry of MCC over the years have been to LGBT families in distress. Sometimes, just like in all families, adults who can hardly manage to take care of themselves are trying to raise and take care of children. MCC churches often function as all large extended families do—they help celebrate victories and bail each other out in crises. The crises of gay and lesbian families are often exacerbated by all the self-esteem challenges associated with coming out; and with trying to become whole and healthy, in our LGBT bodies, minds, and spirits.

Hospitality as a Central Biblical Ethic

Hospitality was essential in a desert culture, especially a nomadic one. In biblical times, if you traveled anywhere in the Near East, you had to depend on the kindness of strangers and acquaintances alike. You had to treat the sojourner well because you might need to depend on someone yourself in the future. There was a common appreciation of the true vulnerability and fragility of life in a desert climate. *It was not a moral choice to be inhospitable.* To do so was to violate the deepest commitment to being human and in community.

The Last Supper is the only dinner where it appears to me as if Jesus is really the host. He makes arrangements for this dinner with his friends and disciples. We have to assume that others actually cooked the food and served it, but Jesus has somehow arranged for this meal to occur. And the reinterpretation of the meal is a very powerful experience of bodily hospitality.

Jesus reinterprets Passover for the disciples at this meal he is hosting. Jesus linked the story of the deliverance of the Jews from slavery to his own life and ministry and death. Jesus proposed a way for this new beloved community of Jews and Gentiles, slave and free, male and female, to embody freedom together, for the healing of the world. Furthermore, they are the guests of the savior. He is feeding them literally, as he has been feeding them spiritually all along. And he uses food and a meal to symbolize his relationship to them now and in the future. In fact, he asks them to think of him in the future whenever they share a meal together, whenever they eat bread and drink wine. Jesus' choice of symbols for himself are very provocative, sensual, and imbued with the images of hospitality.

Jesus asks his guests to ingest him, the reality of his life and death and teachings and being. They are to ingest his healing presence. This is a very risky image.

It certainly risks, at that time and at any time, being associated with cannibalism. But we do not feed on the dead body of Jesus at communion. We are invited to take him into ourselves, not as a dead martyr but as a risen, victorious savior. We are invited to eat and drink from the endless supply of the energy of God that was and is incarnated in the Body of Christ. This imagery is also very sexual, in a nonsexual context. It is sexual in a positive sense—it is about Jesus' own bodily hospitality toward us. The giving of himself physically, spiritually, and emotionally is connected to sexuality in the broadest sense of the word.

Only a Jesus vulnerable enough to be taken could give authentically. I think Jesus shared the gift of human sexuality in a poignant, sweet, metaphysical way at the Last Supper. He invited his followers into a permanent union with him, through bodily symbols of giving and taking. He was preparing for an ultimate act of hospitality—his own suffering and death for their sake, for God's sake, and for the sake of the integrity of the mission. He was willing to open up his body and spirit to suffering and pain, to sacrifice, and to the possibilities of resurrection.

Sexuality, Strangers, and Bodily Hospitality

If my body is my home, then my decision to share my body with another person is a lot like my decision to share my home. The process includes developing a strong sense of what it means to have responsibility for my home. I have to work on developing a sense of my identity as a body/self, including a sense of having *ownership* and responsibility for my own body.

Some of us need to heal a great deal from the ways in which we were alienated from our bodies—or from what we went through just in order to *gain* a sense of independence for our body/self.

I believe that to share ourselves sexually is to give and receive bodily hospitality. Hospitality, to me, can function as a helpful metaphor for ethical sexual relating, which honors the self and the other.

To share sexually with someone is literally to *make* room for that person in your body and in the space surrounding your two bodies. Quite literally, in most forms of sexual intimacy, we enter each other's bodies in some fashion. Whether through kissing, especially deep kissing, various forms of penetration, or holding and stroking playfully or passionately, we have entered the most physically private and protected areas of each other's body/self. And to use the AIDS phrase that has so *clinicized* the nature of sexual activity, we often "exchange bodily fluids." Those are fluids produced from within us, that we manufacture, and they constitute another way in which we have contact with each other's bodies.

I have done a good deal of couples counseling. It seems to me that sometimes people who are married to each other or who are in a long-term committed relationship hardly know each other. They are long-term strangers.

I remember one couple I counseled for a holy union many years ago. They had been together for nine years and had *never had a fight*—not even an argument or a cross word. It was hard to stay in the room with all that buried rage. I tried to tell them that it would probably be a good idea if they learned how to trust each other enough to fight, because otherwise, when they finally did have a fight, it was going to be too big to put back together again. Several months later, their first fight nearly killed one of them, and it ended the relationship *and* the friendship.

And not all "anonymous" sex is really all that *anonymous*. I want to be careful not to romanticize here. I have had very little experience in my own life with sex with strangers. The few experiences I've had were almost all (with two exceptions) pretty disastrous as far as the sex was concerned, and I may be mostly to blame for that! One of the experiences was enjoyable sexually but was terrifying for other reasons, as should become apparent.

My first year of being out of the closet was full of new and dramatic experiences. I fell in love and had sex with someone for the first time in my life. And, like most lesbians, I thought that meant we were married—for life! I moved to Boston, found MCC, and started pastoring while going to seminary full time and working nights in a hospital as a nurse's aide. I worked with dying patients, never imagining that, years later, I would need to recall all that learning. I became a public queer and was temporarily alienated from my parents and family. I cut my hair. I wore a clerical collar for the first time, and people called me "Pastor."

When I went home for a few days at Easter in 1973 to try to talk to my parents (or while they tried to talk to me), my partner had an affair with a young lesbian choir director at MCC Boston. (We were all young in our early twenties) She moved out of our apartment. I was beside myself. I was emotionally dependent on her. I also was terrified of being single or even thinking about dating. I felt like a failure—like I was a rotten lover or partner. I hated being dumped. I begged to be taken back. I threw myself into schoolwork and church with a vengeance.

One night, I thought I'd better try to go out and at least meet some lesbians. So I went to a mixed bar on Boylston Street. I had two drinks, which was one too many for me. I was feeling lonely, desperate, and very angry. And who should appear but the choir director who, by the way, had dumped my now ex-lover after two weeks! (My ex, however, had not failed to mention that those were two weeks of *great* sex.)

Melanie, the choir director (not her real name), approached me all drunk and flirty. A fantasy of revenge concocted itself in my vulnerable state. I'll show her (meaning my ex)! Rules about pastors or assistant pastors sleeping with volunteer music directors were nonexistent in our new world order at that time. But I really did know better. Nevertheless, I was so hurt, needy, curious, flattered, and angry that I followed her to her car and to her bed.

Melanie was the second person I'd ever had sex with, and I'm pretty sure she didn't know that. She was in control, and it was hot, vigorous, adventurous sex. It was as if my sexual imagination had been hermetically sealed until that moment! It excited, frightened, overwhelmed, and exhausted me. In later years, I would come to associate the frenetic, almost insatiable quality of her sexual energy with women who were incest survivors—there was no relaxing or ebb and flow of energy.

Suddenly, at six in the morning, Melanie startled me awake and pushed me out of the bed. As it turned out, her *partner* (which she had not mentioned!) was about to come home from work. Her partner was the owner of the new lesbian bar and the most notorious butch in Boston. I did not want to find out what Maggie would do if she found me in *her* bed, in *her* house with Melanie. I threw on only some of my clothes and ran sneaking out the back door of Maggie's house, praying I would not run into her on her way home and my way back to the train station. Some revenge!

I remember talking to a very young hustler named Bobby years ago, who worked "the block" of a major city. He was trying to explain to me what sex meant to him, especially with these strangers who circled the block mornings and evenings looking for sex from male sex workers. There were the occasional one-time customers, but mostly he had several "regulars," he explained. He told me a very poignant story about one regular. He was a middle-aged man who was quite seriously deformed, so much so that he had special hand controls with which he drove his car. Bobby knew the exact day and time this man would always arrive. When he first met this fellow, he was a little frightened and even turned off by his disability.

The "customer" had explained to Bobby that no "normal" person would voluntarily want to have sex with him, so this was the only way he believed he could have sex with another human being—to pay for it, under circumstances in which he could be endangered or exploited but which had the benefits of certain controls. No danger of emotional pain, for instance—a simple transaction: money for sex. However, with his special needs and circumstances, he preferred to find a hustler he could *count on to show up*. It was very important that he be able to pay for sex. The man did not believe that anyone would enjoy having sex with him, so paying was the only way to ensure that he kept the balance of power. The man was very afraid of being pitied.

Bobby learned a lot from this man—about people with disabilities, about courage and dignity. He began to like him. They talked about *stuff*, stuff other than sex. And they always had sex. Bobby never thought much about the sex when it was going on—with any of his customers. Sometimes he enjoyed the physical sensation, sometimes he didn't. He didn't have to. He did it for the money. Actually, he thought he was straight, and he was just doing this so he could eventually move to California.

But something else began to happen. Because of this man's disability, they had to be a little creative sexually. That unhinged something in

Bobby. More than any other customer, Bobby looked forward to seeing him. There was something playful and intimate about their exchange. At one point, Bobby felt bad—like he was enjoying this as much or more than the customer. He felt like he shouldn't be getting paid. One day, he ventured to say that to the man. The man felt enraged, humiliated; he felt somehow that Bobby didn't want him to pay because he felt sorry for him. Bobby tried to tell him that wasn't it. Bobby finally told me that he kind of loved that guy. He was having a lot of feelings. He wondered how this man spent his days and nights. He wished they could go to a movie or have a meal. But Bobby's expression of his feelings frightened the man, who never again returned to the block.

I think of this story as a parable. Jesus might have told it if he lived in our culture. How do we "pay" to get our needs met? How do we sell ourselves? And how do our fears of lack of control or fears of giving and receiving love and intimacy *disable* us as lovers and friends?

The Fear of Strangers

We live in a culture that is riddled with the fear of strangers—and for good reason. Unlike in Jesus' culture, we do not feel we have any obligation to strangers. Strangers are not potential neighbors. They are potential murderers, robbers, or rapists. We do not see *ourselves* as strangers, even when we are. Strangers are a nuisance; they are dangerous.

I remember my father telling the story of seeing a car broken down by the side of the road. A woman was alone in the car, which was disabled by a flat tire. It was winter. My father spoke to her through her closed window and offered to fix her tire if she would let him in the trunk. She was obviously afraid of him. She opened her window just a crack and put the keys through (apparently not realizing that he could then have opened her door with those very keys if he had wanted to!). He fixed her tire, patiently pushed her keys through the crack in the window, and sent her on her way. Then his own car wouldn't start. No one stopped to help him, and he had to walk to the nearest gas station to *get help*. He always laughed at the irony of this story, but he never said that he would not stop to help someone again.

My goddaughter Rechal has always been a great teacher. I remember when she was about four and in preschool. They were learning about not talking to strangers. She was with me in the grocery store, perched in the little seat in the grocery cart. She was trying to figure out this "stranger" business. As we passed people in the grocery store, she would say, "Are you a stranger?"

People would laugh and usually respond by saying, "Yes." Some would add, "But maybe the next time we meet we won't be." Everyone seemed conscious of what she was struggling with. We established that the pharmacist, whom we had seen for a few years, was probably *not* a stranger.

So we think we *can* trust some strangers in certain roles, and maybe they are not total strangers. To children, especially very young ones, nearly *everyone* is a stranger. When a mother holds her infant in her arms for the first time, are they strangers? In one sense, they have known each other for at least several months (depending on how long the pregnancy was, how long the mother knew she was pregnant, and so on). In another sense, they are meeting each other for the first time.

We come into the world, spending our first nine months inside another's body. We are dependent on another's hospitality. Is our sexuality really partially a longing to renew that kind of intimate interdependence, that first experience of living inside another, safe and welcomed (perhaps)? How does that experience shape our sexuality, and in what way?

But all children arrive as strangers. These are strangers that we are mostly *not* afraid of because they are so small. But some new parents are *very* afraid of the demands, the needs, and the reality of this new, strange little life. We do have to get to know our children. They have their own personalities, their own uniqueness. We cannot *assume* we know them.

How confusing it must be for children to learn of our distrust of strangers when they are themselves so new, so unknown to us, and when there are so few people known to them. But we learn. We learn to ignore strangers, not to see them, especially if they are unusual, physically different, or needy in any way. Adults can walk by and not hear people begging, or see people with deformities or unusual clothes. Children, on the other hand, have to be taught not to notice. We adults are often embarrassed when children just say what they see, talk about what they notice. First we stop saying. Then we stop noticing. The "stranger" business that did not make sense to Rechal that day does not make sense to me and never has.

Rechal knew that, to get along in school, she had to meet strangers and get to know them. Every new teacher was a stranger. I think about the message we teach in church and Sunday school: The only way any church can really grow is by seeking out and inviting and welcoming strangers! All week long, strangers call our church for information, direction, counseling, and help. The most powerful experiences that people often have are coming to the church and being welcomed even though they are strangers.

I remember two young men who called, desperate, because a friend had died. A "community church" (not MCC) up the street in a very gay neighborhood was cold to them and said they didn't let strangers use their church. We not only let them use our church but we let them use it for free. We helped them set up and clean up and provided greeters to assist them. This became the beginning of an important relationship with those men.

MCC pastors have to struggle with these issues. We have to be sensible, but we often have to take chances in meeting strangers. I've gone to the homes of many people who are dying; sometimes I've gone alone, sometimes with other church members. I almost never think about my safety. I think about how to help without being intrusive, what it means to enter someone's home for the first time because he or she—or a partner, friend, or child is dying.

I also meet strangers who come to us because they're in love and want to be married, have a commitment ceremony, or have a baby baptized or dedicated. Inviting strangers into our circles of friendship and love and acceptance is what a healthy, open church experience is about. Yet this is so counter to everything that our culture is teaching us about the fear of strangers.

The process of creating friends from strangers is one of the most fundamental human experiences. Jesus talked again and again about how we might find ourselves in need someday, and wouldn't we want the stranger to behave as if he or she was our neighbor (the Good Samaritan—Luke 10:29–37). Jesus spent his life and ministry touching and being touched by strangers, some of whom loved him, followed him, cared for him, fed him, anointed him, and touched him deeply. Others also betrayed and denied him, beat and crucified him. Some strangers refused his invitation, including one stranger whom it says Jesus *loved*. It is a strange thing to say that one *loves* a stranger, but it says that of Jesus. What did he love about that person? This was someone who had everything but was unsatisfied, longing for a deeper relationship with God. Did Jesus identify with this young man's search, his longing? Was it some mysterious sense of connection or communion in the moment?

I've been attracted to some strangers in my life. For various reasons, perhaps, Jesus was attracted to something in this man and called it love. But I've also even felt sometimes that I loved strangers. Sometimes, when people come to communion at MCC, I have that experience. People whom I've *never* seen before, whose names I do not know, come to me for Holy Communion, to share the Body and Blood of Christ—the most intimate of all Christian sacraments. I don't know a thing about them or what draws them to the table or to this ritual.

Most of the time, if I don't recognize the people who come to communion, I'll ask them their names. I started doing this early on at MCC. I thought it was important, especially for LGBT people, to hear their names at the communion rail *as* they received the Body of Christ, to know that it was for *them* and that God and I wanted to know them. I wanted to know at least their names. Sometimes, someone may look especially troubled or needy, and I have asked that person if he or she needed a special prayer for some reason.

People come to the communion rail quite vulnerable, emotionally and spiritually. They automatically trust that the persons serving are trustable, know what they are doing, and will not only not harm them but will minister to them. Sometimes they get more than they asked for; sometimes, I'm sure, they get less.

Communion with strangers is a very important part of our Sunday worship and daily church experience. I think about what it means for me to pray for strangers, to touch them, to feed them, sometimes to hug them, to say their names. And, more often than not, I find myself loving them with a love that is more than me. I know it is God's love through me loving them. This is a humbling and wonderful experience, as is having a stranger willing to accept that love from me.

It is sensual and bodily in the most innocent and non-exploitative way. We exchange bodily fluids at our communion rail—tears, sometimes perspiration, and the Blood of Christ. I have jokes with my congregation sometimes about how my vestments get a lot of wear and tear. By the end of the day, my vestments and sometimes my shirts and jackets have accumulated tears (and sometimes a little snot for good measure), sweat, and make-up as people have cried with me—laughed, touched, hugged, and kissed me—especially all day Sunday. Add to that the sticky fingers of children and, if we have a class, chalk dust, and I go home with a pile of laundry needing to be done. The experience is at once extremely holy, tactile, and demanding. It is a way in which I can provide bodily hospitality to strangers and friends, colleagues, and family alike. It is a way in which I sometimes feel a profound solidarity with Jesus and with these strangers as well.

And sometimes the strangers themselves are angels. People show up all the time at the church who appear mentally ill, lost, or needy, not even caring what *kind* of church we are. Some of them are hard to deal with; very few are ever really dangerous. Some of them occasionally bring great gifts of all sorts. I've been prayed for in unbelievable ways by them. Some offer just a smile, or a perspective, or a joke. Sometimes, I feel like they are themselves a test for me—especially when they show up on a bad day. Sometimes, I feel like they are wasting my time and energy. But, when I really think about it, they are *not* the ones who have really wasted my time and energy.

Isn't the fear of strangers really the basis of racism and homophobia? They are based on fear of those who are different from us in some way. And, if we all start out as strangers, isn't the fear of strangers really the fear of intimacy, of getting close, and of being vulnerable? Is this why we have had to find ways to separate sexuality and intimacy? Are we so afraid of our own longings and desires for connection, for closeness, that we have developed a whole culture of fear for strangers? I believe that the unhindered gospel that Jesus embodied calls us to overcome those fears.

If it is true that the issues of human sexuality constitute a "seismic fault" that is threatening to divide Christians and the Christian church, how are Jesus' life, ministry, and teachings useful to us in either easing the tension along the fault or practicing "earthquake preparedness?"

I believe that it is extremely difficult for modern people to understand how controversial Jesus was in his time and why. For too many of us, 2,000 years of Christian teaching have put us to sleep with a "Jesus meek and mild" so that we appear to be worshipping a *nice guy who finished last.* The sharp and shocking message and practice that Jesus instituted are lost in the layers of sentimentality. He has been co-opted and normalized, especially by the majority and those in power.

It is useful to compare Jesus' Sabbath controversy with our controversy about human sexuality. This analogy I *believe* will help us understand Jesus' purpose and our dilemma.

What Exactly Was the Sabbath?

Many scholars have tried to discover ancient antecedents to the Hebrew Sabbath. Essentially, the Sabbath was a weekly festival in which Israel's relationship to God was honored and remembered. The Sabbath was about rest. Tradition said that God had created the world in six days and rested on the seventh. It was a celebration of creation itself. Israel was to *imitate* God and honor God by resting on the Sabbath. It was a time for worship and recreation.

The Sabbath was also connected to the experience of the Exodus. Israel *could* rest because they were no longer slaves. Slaves had to work seven days a week. But they had been delivered by a God who did not believe they should be slaves to anything, including work. They were to rest on the Sabbath as a sign of their freedom, as well as a sign of their partnership with God in creation.

Over the centuries, the Sabbath grew in its significance. It began to have political as well as religious meaning. "Keeping the Sabbath" became a primary sign of being a Jew. It was a sign of national identity. Other nations were aware of this peculiar custom among the Jews. Nations sometimes, in fact, used this information to gain an advantage over them. There are many stories in the Bible and the Apocrypha of Israel being attacked on the Sabbath. In some of these stories, God comes to their rescue. In other stories, Jews are martyred for their observation of the Sabbath. This becomes, by Jesus' time, a considerable historical legacy.

There were many in Jesus' time whose ancestors had died rather than defile the Sabbath. Keeping the Sabbath was an essential part of showing that you were a loyal Jew, that you were proud of your heritage, that you loved God, and that you were in touch with your history and your people.

In addition, the Sabbath was already being mystified, as in the concept of the "Sabbath bride." In Jewish Sabbath worship, the Sabbath is welcomed into the synagogue as a bride into the bridal chamber. It is a lovely, embodied, holy, and sensuous image. The Sabbath is the bride of Israel, much as the church is the "bride of Christ" in the New Testament. There was a sense of a mystical union between the concept of the Sabbath and the concept of Jewishness.

Sabbath preparations could be simple or elaborate, as they may be today. The preparation and the celebration were a part of the holistic understanding of faith: faith includes one's heart, mind, body, and spirit. The Sabbath observance required participation of all of these in study, prayers, food, rest, family, and home.

The Sabbath provided a wonderful weekly reminder of the important things in a person's life. In our contemporary secularized culture, both the Jewish Sabbath and the Christian Sabbath are fading fast from the scene. We live in times of excesses, of 24-hour stores and restaurants, of workaholism, of slavery to work and profit, of the disappearance of leisure time. The days of regular mealtimes for families, of weekly play and recreation times, or of worshipping together are disappearing. Life's rhythms are highly frenetic. For many people, there is no Sabbath, no rest, and no holy time of stopping to pray or relax, make love, or take time over a meal with friends.

Our modern Sabbath-free life is the nightmare the ancient rabbis feared. A society without rest is one without God, without health, and without balance.

The Sabbath was also the means of expression of identity. Not to keep the Sabbath is to forget who you are. Cultural and religious notions of identity are located in the celebration of feasts and holidays.

We experienced this with the Latin ministry at Metropolitan Community Church Los Angeles. Even though many of the participants in the Spanish-language service at ten in the morning also speak English, it is so comforting and identity-building for many people to worship in an MCC *in the Spanish language*. It gives the lie to the claim that LGBT people are primarily white, Anglo, and not from Catholic backgrounds. Also, Latin ministry leaders have struggled to preserve the varied Latin American cultures in our life as a community. For instance, Protestants and Catholics celebrate Holy Week differently and with different intensities. This is compounded by the fact that, in many Latin countries, from Holy Thursday at Noon through Easter, no one works. It is a prolonged Sabbath. Many Latin people feel quite alienated when life goes on as usual during Holy Week in the United States, even if the church has services every evening or all day Sunday.

Also, we had the *palms* issue. Most Protestants in the U.S. hand out palms on Palm Sunday, and they are pitiful little things. Often, they are just little strips of palm leaves that Sunday school children fold into the shape of a cross and pin on their clothing. That, for us, is Palm Sunday.

The first Palm Sunday that the Latin ministry held a service, they were dumbfounded. Palms for Palm Sunday in their experience were huge palm branches that the church members waved as they processed with them into the sanctuary. The next year we had to order two different kinds of palms.

And, sometimes, it is a matter of food or how one throws a party. All of these factors contribute to a sense of tradition, peoplehood, identity, comfort, and home.

In our church, we have two "layers" of tradition. The first is what we bring with us from our ethnic or denominational background. This is what we want to preserve, especially if it helps others feel more at home and welcome at MCC. Some people, still dealing with severe internalized homophobia, wonder if we are a "real" church. They look for signs, some of which are as simple as *Does this experience look, sound, smell, and feel like church* (meaning churches they attended or grew up in)? We have to preach frequently about helping people let go of *some* of these associations in order to free them from negative aspects of their past religious experience or to make room for others. The second layer, that I'll deal with in a little bit, is the tradition we create.

Ethnic signs and signals are another matter, also complicated. We're not a melting pot; we're more like a tossed salad in that regard. But we have to negotiate frequently about how "user friendly" we are in a cultural sense, for many kinds of people and cultures.

Marlene came to MCC Los Angeles one Pentecost Sunday in May. I had met her nearly 18 months before and had been waiting for her to show up. I had spoken at a group on coming out, and she had been a participant. We had connected, and I knew she was filled with religious conflicts. She wanted to come to church but might have a hard time getting there.

It was a gorgeous day, and I was waiting in the small vestibule at Crescent Heights Methodist Church (we were meeting there during the early days of renovation of our church property). I smiled and said, "Good morning, Marlene." She was shocked that I remembered her or her name. But I had remembered. I remembered the intensity, the need. I had prayed for her, and I smiled at her and at the satisfaction of answered prayer.

It was nearly six months before we discovered the importance of Marlene's arrival at MCC on Pentecost. She did not know it was Pentecost.

But later on she told me how, as a little Portuguese Catholic child, her most precious *religious* memories were of an annual Portuguese religious festival. There were always parties, wonderful food, and a big parade through the small northern California immigrant town she grew up in. Each year, a little girl was chosen to be the *queen of this parade,* honoring the Virgin Mary. The festival was a religious and cultural one, in which Marlene took pride. Her fondest memory was of the year she had been chosen to be the queen of the parade, at about age ten. With all the negative and oppressive memories of church and childhood, this festival and her *one* moment of glory stood out in contrast. It was something precious that she had kept alive in her heart—a precious Sabbath experience.

Later, she would feel as though that joyful, loved feeling she remembered from the festival connected to her experience of God at MCC Los Angeles. She came home to herself in a gay and lesbian church experience that accepted all of who she was—lesbian, Catholic, and Portuguese.

I remember the moment that she was able to tell me that the Portuguese festival was on the feast of *Pentecost.* I reminded her that her first Sunday at MCC Los Angeles (and her first really adult experience of going to church, at age 40) was also Pentecost. It was as if her mind and body and spirit knew exactly when to return to church. She returned on the very Sabbath day that represented the most affirming, powerful, positive experience of God she had ever had.

This experience, this *coincidence,* was an important part of Marlene's spiritual journey. She had an agenda and a timetable. Marlene had cancer. She came to the church seeking physical and spiritual healing.

A little over two years after that Pentecost, Marlene died of breast cancer. She always expressed her hope for both kinds of healings, but rejoiced that she lived long enough to experience a healed, renewed, and joy-filled relationship with God. She learned how to pray, she bought her own Bible, and became a virtual "church mouse," present nearly every time the doors were open and when she felt well enough to come. She basked in the freedom to think and feel and pray to the God of her own heart and understanding, like a child welcomed home after a glorious parade. The memory of her still blesses us at Pentecost and throughout the year.

We have lots of homegrown traditions. Often, we do something once, and the next year it becomes a "tradition." We invent these customs and celebrate yearly events because they provide a sense of linkage,

144 • Outing the Church

connection, and reliability in a very unreliable world. Also, many of the old traditions have such painful associations that we need at least to redefine them, if not reinvent them, for ourselves. Plus, we express ourselves, our own culture, and our own history through these new traditions. This is one way in which we get to tell the stories again and again of how we have survived and triumphed. It is how we keep the Sabbath.

Just suppose that, like the Sabbath, sexuality is a gift from God! There are lots of churches today that say this is the basis of their theological understanding of sexuality. They say "sexuality," but they mean heterosexuality, or, as I have heard it labeled, *heteronormativity*.[28] Let's face it: for much of the history of Christian thought and practice, sexuality has not been preached about, or taught about, as if it were a gift at all. Historically, sexuality was seen, at best, as a necessary evil—something humankind *has to do* if it is going to continue to exist. Sexuality was to be controlled and policed (like the Sabbath). It was dangerous. Women embodied sexual lust, and men could easily become "prey" to its temptations. Sexism particularly poisoned our view of sexuality. Repression and obsession became the pattern we are still stuck with today.

I can imagine God's fury about this. I see how angry God is at the way the story of Adam and Eve was distorted to mean that sex and the Fall are synonymous. The Sabbath, a gift of God, became a primary way Jews could break the law and sin. That is very similar to the way in which sexuality is rarely seen, in a Christian context, as a means of grace but as the primary occasion for sin.

We are a mess about sex, and the churches have helped create this mess—and they have not only not helped us to heal but they continue to hurt. I think of the parade of television evangelists, mega-church leaders, and famous gospel singers who have repressed their God-given, sexual orientation, only to be caught in compromising situations—or worse—in exploitive situations.

Too often, they pathetically confess and "repent," going even deeper into their denial. That pattern characterizes so much of our sexual culture. For me, the startling truth is that judgmental, anti-LGBT preaching is as misguided as the sexual adventures. The preaching, the condemnation, and the lies fuel this lust and deceit. Church members from all walks of life are longing for a deep, embodied sexual connectedness in their lives. Instead, they are fed lies.

In 1993, Jerry Falwell, one of the first television evangelists to make his career on the backs of LGBT people, created a video called *The Gay Agenda*, a video that features footage from the 1993 gay and lesbian march on Washington. An ad he created made it sound like porn. "It's so [disgusting] that you can't show it to children," he says several times as he smirks. He gives a few "sneak previews" of the footage they have, some of which, of course, features the more campy and outrageous participants in the gay march.

Today, as anti-LGBT evangelicals are losing the battle here in the United States, they have exported this hate and salaciousness to places like Uganda. Scott Lively went to Uganda in 2009 in support of his book, *The Pink Swastika*, in which he blames the Nazi holocaust on gay men. In Uganda, he exported the old lies of gay men wanting to have sex with boys and animals.[29] He met with Ugandan Parliament members, and not long afterwards the infamous "Anti-Homosexuality Bill" proposed the death penalty for gay people and imprisonment for anyone who refused to report them.[30] Ugandan Pastor Martin Ssempa actually shows gay porn to adults and children to perpetrate a hyper-sexualized caricature of all gay men. With this as the foundation, the *New York Times* op-doc closes with a scene in which a speaker asks hundreds of listeners, "Those who are ready to kill those who are doing homosexual, hands up!" All hands went up.[31]

For many fundamentalists, the orgy of confessing and repenting, the fanaticism, and the rhetoric are all either a *defense* against unacceptable sexual feelings, or they actually provide a *substitute experience* for them. For Catholics, I see a tremendous polarity here. The vast majority ignore the Catholic church's teaching on birth control that is contained in endless books, pamphlets, and Vatican pronouncements. Most Catholics see the religious police in this issue as irrelevant and give them no power. In Mexico, I found that contraceptives were more visible in grocery stores than even in drugstores in the United States. Most Catholics do *not* believe what the church says God wants from them vis-a-vis birth control. But the church still has a lot of power to shame the divorced, homosexuals, or anyone who doesn't conform to other rules that the church claims are God's laws.

On the Sabbath, the divine and the earthly were not to be polarized, but were to come together, to be married, and to be in harmony. The Sabbath was the bride of Israel. Our sexuality is a gift from God. It is not meant to be something about which we are tormented and tortured, or with which we torture and torment others. It was meant to be one of the primary ways in which we experience connection with God and God's purpose in creation. Our sexuality, rightly lived and celebrated, is to draw us closer to God, not to drive us away from Eden. Millennialist theology claims that, in a renewed Eden, sexual happiness will be our portion. Sexuality is to be a joyful component of Eden, not what drives us away.

At one point in our stormy relationship, I teased the National Council of Churches of Christ in the U.S.A. I said, "Do you know where I see the greatest unhappiness about sexuality in the world today? Not in the gay and lesbian community. Not in the prisons or hospitals I visit. Not even in the streets. The greatest unhappiness about sexuality I see is at *meetings of the National Council of Churches*."[32] And by that I meant that sometimes I felt as if MCC should have a counseling room at the meetings. Often we did, but it was my hotel room or the hotel rooms of other MCC visitors at the NCC. Sometimes, we counseled in hallways or doorways. People would seek us out to talk about their gay son or daughter or their child with AIDS. We talked with men who were gay but couldn't tell their wives. A heterosexually married staff person's lover died of AIDS, but he could tell no one. He sobbed in my arms in the corner of a meeting room. Men and women whose marriages were troubled for other reasons would choose *us* to talk to. I held governing board members in my arms who cried about their divorces or the struggles of being widowed. Some harbored shameful secrets or sought us out with painful questions. Some came to me wanting to know if I thought that so-and-so was gay.

Others knocked on our doors late at night, hoping to God no one saw them. Some people would never be caught *dead* talking to me, not realizing that that in itself was a dead giveaway.

I could always tell who the gay or lesbian or bisexual people were at a conference with the "pamphlet test." We would put out our pamphlets on a table with other literature. People would glance at them, some would pick them up to peruse them, and some would take copies. But if a person saw our literature and *then looked furtively* over his or her shoulder ("Were any religious police lurking nearby?") before putting it down or taking it, I knew he or she was struggling with shame or guilt. I knew he or she was probably gay or lesbian, bisexual or transgender.

Some people were cruel and judgmental, asking inappropriate and prying questions they would never ask of a heterosexual person or wish to be asked themselves. There were people who knocked on our doors late at night looking for sex. Others came on to us at the dinner table, or *under* the dinner table, or sitting next to us on a bus on the way to an NCC event. We dealt with men who thought lesbian meant "hard to get" or that it meant we were bisexual or liked "three-ways" or that we were open to "kinky" sex. We who were supposed to be *worldly* and sophisticated about such matters found ourselves shocked at times, amused, and sometimes not amused.

Some folks would proposition us for sex and then vote against us on the floor of National Council of Churches of Christ meetings. They were self-hating homosexuals, bisexuals, or heterosexuals experimenting while away from home. Sometimes the temptation to "out" these folks was nearly more than we could bear.

It also seemed to me that NCC meetings were, in general, very unsexy. They were dull, controlled, and often devoid of much passion. As young people, feminists, and social justice advocates faded from the scene, the meetings became even less "sexy."

I use the word "sexy" here literally (as in not many people acted like they were in touch with their own sexuality in a joyous way) and symbolically, as in *interesting* or *exciting!* It was as if *we* from MCC provided the "sexual energy" for the meeting. We were called on for late-night meetings and conferences at the hotel *bar* until two in the morning. Confessions, intrigue, negotiations, capitulations, attempts at co-opting (seduction!), rage, grief, and feeling of any kind seemed mostly to happen in relationship to our presence. It was a way in which I sometimes personally felt exploited. It took years for me to understand this. We were their avenue for sexual projection and excitement. It was *not very good* for us, however!

Harassment aside, most of what we did at NCC meetings was to listen to people and to love them and try to keep our own boundaries, perspectives, and self-esteem. What sadness to witness all of this pain and struggle over the gift of sexuality! And then the National Council of Churches of Christ would continue to act terribly wounded that we were *forcing* them to deal with these controversial issues, as if it had nothing to do with them!

A group of Presbyterians, in the context of trying one more time to find a way to help the church work through its issues about gays and lesbians, suggested that the church needs a new basis for sexual ethics called *justice/love.*[33] The furor that this suggestion caused would make an excellent study in the sexual pathology of the church. But justice/love is exactly what Jesus was saying about the Sabbath. The Sabbath was made for us, not us for the Sabbath. Sexuality is a gift for us; we were not created to serve an outdated, oppressive, and sick sexual ethic. How can we, in the spirit of Jesus, restore and reform sexuality, as he attempted to do with the Sabbath?

Sometimes, when churches study "human sexuality," this is just a euphemism for wanting to study *homosexuality*. Other times, the term "human sexuality" is a way to *avoid* talking about homosexuality—as if, of course, homosexuality was not human! When churches, for instance, proclaim that they really do believe that human sexuality is a gift from God, they *do not* also affirm that gay and lesbian sexuality is a gift from God. In the early days (the early 1980s) of our application to the National Council of Churches of Christ in the United States, the most troubling MCC declaration was that homosexuality, as a component of human sexuality, is a gift from God.

Sexuality is, or should be, a great equalizer. "Love belongs to everyone, The best things in life are free," says the old song.[34] Sex, of course, is not always free, and it is not always, or perhaps even mostly, about love. It has become commodified and can be very costly. Unsafe sex, these days especially, is costing billions of dollars and may end up costing millions of lives.

Sex tourism also compromises the ideal of sexuality as a great equalizer. Many Asian countries, in particular, have become economically dependent on the sex tourism trade to such a degree that they *cannot* safeguard the health of their people (especially women and children) or their blood supply without causing economic hardships. This is an extreme global example of the eroticization of dependency, and it is causing tremendous suffering, shame, loss, and death. Human traffickers, for sex and/or labor, enslave 27 million people worldwide.

With the generations of sex abuse in churches coming to light, this projection of immorality on "others" reveals a desperate need for sexual healing—not only for those who have been assaulted but for every person who feels shame about his or her sexuality.

What would it mean to provide a "safe space" in which to deal with the volatile issues that sexuality raises? The concept of the Sabbath is in many ways related to the concept of sanctuary. It expresses in time what *sanctuary* communicates in terms of space. The church needs a Sabbath, a sanctuary, in some corner where it can rest, relax, and take all the time and space it needs to recover its integrity as a place of justice, love, and safety for all people.

Jesus healed on the Sabbath. Interestingly, he did not heal people on the Sabbath only as a matter of life and death. There was a provision for that in the laws (there were all kinds of emergency provisions). But Jesus wanted to *normalize* healing on the Sabbath and to point out that it should not have to be an emergency, a matter of life and death. Any good done on the Sabbath should enhance the meaning and purpose of the Sabbath. So he healed a man with a withered hand, someone he could just as easily have healed the next day. He said, in effect, "It's my Sabbath, and I'll heal if I want to." If the purpose of the Sabbath was to provide wholeness, balance, joy, and connectedness to God as a standard feature of one's life and week, then how was healing someone ever a violation of that understanding?

How is the gift of sexuality connected to healing? We certainly know that touch itself is healing. What if our sexual ethic were based on what *good* or *harm* sex accomplished, not on what rules we followed? Touch that happens in massage or by being stroked or petted, or by stroking or petting another (including a pet, for instance!) actually lowers our blood pressure and increases our mental and physical health! We all learned in science classes about the infants who were deprived of touch (while they were well fed and clothed and otherwise cared for). Touch deprivation caused a *failure to thrive,* which meant that some of them died. People are dying emotionally and spiritually, if not also physically, because they are not touched. Some people have learned ways to trade sexual "favors" for touch. This is tragic, sick, and sad. People should be able to have their touch and sexual needs met, together or independently, without having to trade, sell, manipulate, or be deprived.

I know that coming out as a lesbian and a sexual person was one of the most *healing* events in my life. It seems to me that that is true for many, if not most, gay and lesbian people. Contrary to what some have said, I do not believe that most gays and lesbians would prefer to be straight; we would *all* prefer to have the stigma removed from our sexuality, but I can recall meeting only a few gay men (and no lesbians that I can recall) who have wished they were heterosexual.

For some people, it is only the guilt and shame that precedes their coming out that are so painful. For some, the first sexual experience of any kind is overwhelming, frightening, and mixed with pleasure and pain. For most LGBT people to whom I have talked, their first *homosexual* experiences were confirming and included a sense of great relief, of coming home to their body—to their true feelings and nature. Sometimes, the first sexual experience also included coming home to a new community.

I remember the occasion when my oldest niece came by herself for the first time to visit Paula and me. I told my brother that he had to tell her I am a lesbian because the chances were that, if she came to church or was around our godchildren for any length of time, she would hear the word. And I wanted her to know, from her dad, that *he* knew and that there were certain vocabulary and information words that she would need to know, which would help her feel more included. I think he did do that, but perhaps he used the word *gay,* not *lesbian,* and I'm not sure that what he said really registered with this ten-year-old. At one point, my niece and goddaughter Rechal and I were at lunch when Rechal decided to make some statements about lesbians. "What's a *lesbian?*" said my niece.

"Well," I said, "it's like your dad explained to you [hoping he had]. Sometimes men are with women, sometimes men are with men, and sometimes women are with women."

She pondered this a moment. Perhaps she wasn't quite sure I meant what she *thought* I meant by the preposition (which functions a lot like a verb in those phrases!) *with.* Then she said, "So, how did you and Aunt Paula meet?" Bingo. I knew she had gotten it. We had had to *meet* somewhere just like her mom and dad had *met.* How did *they* (homosexuals) do that, anyway?

All things being equal, gay folk could just speak freely with heterosexuals about how we meet, date, fall in love, fall out of love, decide to move in together, make commitments, share children and in-laws, and decide actually to have children. These are really not profound mysteries. Mostly, they are not exotic tales.

Almost always, when I do counseling for holy union ceremonies for LGBT couples, when I ask them how they met, they giggle. I've done quite a number of heterosexual weddings as well, and no straight couple has ever giggled when I asked them how they met. Maybe it is because, for the queer couple, meeting each other often coincides with one or both of them coming out. Or it brings up the anxiety all of us feel when we either venture into the gay world or discover each other in a heterosexual environment ("Is she or isn't she? I think she is; she never mentions a boyfriend, and she plays on that softball team"; "he says he has a roommate, is it his lover or just a roommate; whom can I ask?")

Equality could mean that no one would assume that a particular child is going to be heterosexual. That children would be aware early on that whatever their orientation (whether they think of it as a discovery or a choice), their choice of partner or partners is not going to determine whether or not they have a right to live, breathe, feel, speak openly, live with whom they choose, work in a profession they have prepared for, keep their children with them, have a right to survivor benefits, be on their spouse's insurance policy, or be buried with their loved ones. Equality would mean that I am included at some basic assumptive level in the consciousness of a culture, including its politics and spirituality. It would mean that I am not permanently an "other," outside of the normal considerations and always an intrusive *exception,* which is what makes us appear to be flaunting our sexuality. I think the opposite of flaunting is disappearing—the *secret wish that we would simply go away and die.*

But we are not going away—not voluntarily and not at all. We are a necessary and essential part of creation and of every people and every culture. Sometimes honored, sometimes vilified, we are very often those who travel first to the enigmatic borders of cultures and millennia. We are often the "scouts" who see the future approaching and who beckon or warn. Our planet needs a Sabbath in this time of cultural and millennial shifts. We need that time-out in which to reflect, to repent, and to ask the deepest questions about what we want this new millennium to offer our children and grandchildren.

What if, in our new charter of human existence, we come to believe that all people have a right to a Sabbath, and a right to be who they are spiritually and sexually? And that all life forms deserve to be respected? What a powerful millennial vision!

Notes

1   See Susan Thistlewaite, *Sex, Race, and God: Christian Feminism in Black and White* (New York: Crossroad, 1991).

2   Rev. Troy Perry, *The Lord Is My Shepherd and He Knows I'm Gay* (Los Angeles: UFMCC Press, 1994), p. 201.

3   The same story is told in Rakesh Ratti's "An Improbable Pair," in *Lotus of Another Color*, ed. by R. Ratti (Boston: Alyson Publications, 1993), pp. 175–89.

4   Transcription of Chris Cowap's remarks to the NCC governing board, November 9, 1983, in Hartford.

5   The Lima Liturgy was proposed by the WCC Commission on Faith and Order and was composed at a conference in Lima, Peru, prior to the 1991 General Assembly. It is the first ecumenical communion liturgy composed and celebrated by such a diverse international Christian body.

6   Emily Dickinson, "I Never Saw a Moor," *The Poems of Emily Dickinson*, ed. by Thomas H. Johnson (Cambridge, Mass.: Belknap Press of Harvard University Press, 1955).

7   Angela Davis, "Rape, Racism, and the Myth of the Black Rapist," in *Women, Race, and Class* (New York: Random House, 1981), pp. 172–201.

8   Presbyterian Church (U.S.A.), *Presbyterians and Human Sexuality* (Louisville, Ky.: Office of the General Assembly, Louisville, 1991), p. 2.

9   M. Scott Peck, *People of the Lie* (New York: Simon and Schuster, 1983).

10 Harry Hay, "A Separate People Whose Time Has Come," in *Gay Spirit*, ed. by Mark Thompson (New York: St. Martin's Press, 1987), pp. 279–91.

11 Freda Smith, "Dear Dora/Dangerous Derek Diesel Dyke," used with permission of the author.

12 Carter Heywood, *Touching Our Strength: The Erotic as Power and the Love of God* (San Francisco: Harper & Row, 1989).

13 Nelle Morton, *The Journey Is Home* (Boston: Beacon Press, 1985), chap. 1, 23.

14 Lucia Chappelle, "Silent Night, Raging Night," in *DeColores MCC Hymnal* (Los Angeles: 1983), p. 6.

15 Mark Thompson, "Children of Paradise: A Brief History of Queens," in *Gay Spirit*, pp. 61–68.

16 Hay, "A Separate People," p. 285.

17 Ibid., p. 280.

18 Harold Kushner, *When Bad Things Happen to Good People* (New York: Shocken Books, 1981); M. Scott Peck, *The Road Less Traveled* (New York: Simon & Schuster, 1978).

19 Stephen Hall, *Mapping the New Millennium* (New York: Vintage Books, 1992).

20 Ibid., p. 95.

21 Ibid., p. 101.

22 Ibid., p. 103.

23 See "Introduction," pp. 3–4.

24 See Tex Sample, *Hard-Living People and Mainstream Christians* (Nashville, Tenn.: Abingdon Press, 1993) for his definition and description of the sociology and spirituality of "hard-living people."

25 Perry, *The Lord Is My Shepherd.*

26 Farley Mowatt, *People of the Deer* (Toronto, Ont.: Seal Books, 1951), pp. 96–109.

27 James Nelson, *Embodiment: An Approach to Sexuality and Christian Theology* (Minneapolis: Augsburg Press, 1978).

28 I have Nathan Meckley to thank for teaching me this word!

29 Excerpts of Scott Lively's 2009 speech in Uganda are available at http://youtube.com/watch?v=amVnWtpR1is.

30 Chris Vogel, "The Crusader," *Boston Magazine*, March 2013 edition. Available at http://bostonmagazine.com/news/article/2013/02/26/scott-lively-anti-gay-uganda-governor.

31 Roger Ross Williams, "Gospel of Intolerance," *New York Times*, January 22, 2013. Available at: http://nytimes.com/2013/01/23/opinion/gospel-of-intolerance.html.

32 From an unpublished speech I gave to the National Council of Churches of Christ in the U.S.A., May 1987.

33 *Presbyterians and Human Sexuality.*

34 B. G. DeSylva, L. Brown, and R. Henderson, "Best Things in Life Are Free," 1927, from the musical *Good News.*

Subject Index

A

abuse, idea of deserved, 62–63
Adams, Lew, 52–53
Adult Children of Alcoholics, 61–62
adult spirituality, 63–64, 66–73
AIDS agencies, 98–99
AIDS demonstration, 54–55, 82–83
Alamo, Tony, 61
Alexander, Michelle, 6
All Saints day student clergy liturgy,
    48–50
angels, 98–100
anointing with oil, 44–46
anonymous sex, 132–135
authoritarian religions, 64

B

Bacon, Ed, 26
berdache, 43
The Bible
    earthquakes in, 76–83
    new lens on, 53–57
biblical theology, tribal structures
    and, 6
bodily differences, 121–130
body
    as home, 119–121
    hospitality, 116, 118–119
        pregnancy, 124
        sexuality and, 131–135

ownership, 118–135
breeders, 19

C

Camp Letts, 36–39
Chappelle, Lucia, 39–40
children
    body ownership, 122
    forbidden contact, 26
    gayby boom, 20–21
    Jessie and Rechal, 22–24
    LGBT people as non-reproductive,
        50–51
    religious experiences, 63–64
    strangers, 136–137
    violence in family of origin, 21
Children of Paradise: A Brief History
    of Queens (Thompson), 40–41
Christmas season, 108–114
church within the church, 36
clergy
    as authority figures, 31
    reactions to female, 103–105
    sexism, 38–39
    sexuality discussions, 30–31
    transference and, 31
coming out as gift, 33–36
communion of saints, 100
communion with strangers, 138
Cowap, Chris, 7–11

D

"Dear Dora/Dangerous Derek Diesel
  Dyke" (Smith), 36
deaths, 101–102, 106–107
  hospice on Christmas, 111–114
demonization, 97
dependency, 36
deserved abuse thinking, 62–63
dominance, 36
Don't Ask, Don't Tell, 15–16
Don't Be Afraid Anymore (Perry), 21

E

earthquakes, 59–61, 69–70
  biblical, 76–83
  faith crises and, 73–74
  fundamentalists and, 61–62
  God and, 61–62
  as good thing, 62
  message, 71–72
  seismic sexuality, 74–76
  Sodom and Gomorrah and, 72
  theological uses, 76–77
  waves, 72
ecumenical movement
  Cowap, Chris, 8, 11
  Eucharist, 11–13
  feminism, 7
emotional poverty, 66–67
enigmatic border, 70–71
eroticism of friendship, 36
Eucharist
  ecumenical, 11–13
  prison ministry, 95
  with strangers, 138
eunuchs, 116
evil, lying and, 35

F

false witness, wounds of, 18–24
Falwell, Jerry, 18, 145

Foye, Jean, 107–108
Frank, Barney, 17
fundamentalism, 5
  earthquakes, 61–62
  prison ministry, 88–95
  sexuality and, 145
  spiritual narcissism and, 64
  in West Hollywood, 55–56

G

gay agenda, 15, 145
gay bars, 83–84, 124–126
gay God, 48–50
gayby boom, 20–21
gifts
  coming out, 33–36
  creativity, 42–46, 50
  humor, 40–42, 47–52
  image of God, 50
  irreverent piety, 51–52
  made in image of God, 46–50
  new lens on the Bible, 53–57
  pro-life spirituality, 50–51
  same-sex eroticism, 36–40, 50
  suffering, uses for, 52–53
  truth telling, 50
go-betweens, 43, 116
God
  gay God, 48–50
  sense of humor, 47
God Box, 7–8
Grahn, Judy, 5

H

Hall, Stephen, 69–70
Hay, Harry, 46
healing, sexuality and, 149–150
heathens, 97
heteronormativity, 144
heterosexist roles, MCC leaders,
  37–38

holidays, 108–114
homoerotic gestures, 28
homophobia, internalized, 50
homosexuality studies, 115, 148
hospice visits on Christmas, 111–114
hospitality
    as biblical ethic, 130–131
    body hospitality, 116, 118–119
    eunuchs and, 116
    gay butlers, 116–117
    Last Supper, 130–131
    lesbians, 117
    queer sensibility and, 116
    strip shows, 127
    Thanksgiving dinner, 117–118
human sexuality as euphemism for
    homosexuality, 148
humor
    gift of, 40–42
    God's, 47
    irreverent piety, 51–52
    Hutton, Kate, 59–61

I

image of God, 46–50
Inclusive Language Lectionary, 9
intercessors, 43
Inter-Church Center Manhattan. See
    God Box
internalized homophobia, 50
irreverent piety, 51–52
Is the Homosexual My Neighbor?
    (Mollenkott and Scanzoni), 18

J

Jack Benny, 3–4
Jessie and Rechal's story, 22–24
Joel, Billy, "Just the Way You Are,"
    47–48
justice, 16–17, 148

K

Kenneth's story, 93
King, Rodney, 16
Kiron and Jerry's story, 6–7
Korean man in Australia, 42
Kushner, Harold, 64

L

Last Supper, hospitality and, 130–131
lezzies, 27–28
liberation theology, 66–67
Lima Liturgy, 11–12
Lively, Scott, 145
Lloyd's story, 102, 105–106
*The Lord Is My Shepherd and He [sic]
    Knows I'm Gay* (Perry), 6
lying, 35

M

mature spirituality, 66–73
MCC (Metropolitan Community
    Churches)
    church for everybody, 20
    healing sexism among women,
    38–39
    heterosexist roles among leaders,
    37–38
    minor children attending, 19
    prison chaplaincy, 90–92
metaphors, 49
military personnel, 15–16
Mollenkott, Virginia, 9, 18

N

Narcissism, spiritual, 61–67
NCC (National Council of Churches
    of Christ)
    Commission on Women in
    Ministry, 7
    dialogue committees on
    homosexuality, 115–116
    unhappiness about sexuality, 146

negative traits passed on, 46
*The New Jim Crow: Mass
Incarceration in the Age of
Colorblindness* (Alexander), 6
Norman, Connie, 54–55

O

oppression comparison, 16
ownership of the body, 121–130

P

Palm Sunday services, 141–142
pamphlet test, 146–147
patriarchy, sexuality and, 25, 36
Paul and Silas and the jailer, 77–82
Peck, Jane Carey, 9–10
Peck, M. Scott, 35, 64
Pentecost, 142–143
Perry, Troy, 6, 21, 84
The Pink Swastika (Lively), 145
poverty, spiritual or emotional,
66–67
Presbyterians and Human Sexuality,
25
prison ministry, 83–95
progressive churches, adult
spirituality and, 64
Project Angel Food, 98
projection, wounds from, 24–32

Q–R

queer millennialist theology, 3, 16–18

religion, authoritarian, 64
religious right
gay agenda and, 15
Ninth Commandment breaking,
18–19
repression, wounds from, 24–32
Ride, Joyce, 86
Rob's story, 3–5
Roger's story, 19–20

S

Sabbath, 140–151
same-sex eroticism as gift, 36–40
Sanford, Agnes, 70
Scanzoni, Letha, 18
seismic sexuality, 74–76
selective holocaust, 101
sex tourism, 148
sexism, healing MCC women, 38–39
sexual projection, 24–25, 102–103
sexuality
author's early impressions, 27–28
body hospitality and, 131–135
churches and, 144–145
enigmatic border of life and
creativity, 70–71
fundamentalism and, 145
as gift from God, 144
healing and, 149–150
MCC clergy and, 30
patriarchy and, 25, 36
Presbyterians and Human
Sexuality, 25
repression and, 26
same-sex eroticism as gift, 36–40
seismic, 74–76
sexual projection and, 25
theology of, 115
unhappiness about, 146
shamanistic gifts, 42–46
Smith, Freda, 36
Sodom and Gomorrah, 72, 116
sodomites, 83–84
softball teams, 46–47
spiritual ancestors, 100
spiritual health, truth and, 35–36
spiritual narcissism, 61–67
spiritual poverty, 66–67
spirituality
adults who stop growing, 63–64
creative use of suffering, 52–53

as enigmatic border between
worlds, 71
mature, 66–73
pro-life, 50–51
spiritualizing the poor, 66–67
sterotypes, 18–25, 43
strangers
anonymous sex and, 132–135
children, 136–137
communion with, 138
couples as, 132
creating friends of, 137–138
fear of, 135–139
homophobia and, 139
racism and, 139
strippers, 125–130
suffering, creative use, 52–53

T

temple of spirit, body as, 118
theological anthropology, 5
Thompson, Mark, 40–41
tribal structures, 6–7, 11–13
trickster's role, 40–41
truth, 34–36
two-spirited people, 31–32

U-V

Ugandan anti-homosexuality bill,
19, 145
violence in family of origin, 21

W

Walker, Thomas, 15–16
WCC (World Council on Churches),
human rights agenda, LGBT
people and, 97–98
*When Bad Things Happen to Good
People* (Kushner), 64
women's prison ministry, 85–89
wounds
of false witness, 18–24
from projection and repression,
24–32

X-Y-Z

Yvonne's story, 86

Scripture Index

1 Samuel 14–15, 77

Psalms 2:4, 47

Amos 1:1, 76

Zechariah 14:5, 76

Matthew 28:2, 77

John 8:32, 34

Acts 16, 77–78
Acts 16:18, 77–78
Acts 16:25–34, 78
Acts 28:31, 77